JOSHUA

REST-LAND WON

To

My brothers and sisters

JOSHUA

REST-LAND WON

By
IRVING L. JENSEN

MOODY PRESS
CHICAGO

ISBN: 0-8024-2006-0

13 14 15 16 Printing/EP/Year 92 91 90 89 88

Printed in the United States of America

CONTENTS

PREFACE

THE AVERAGE CHRISTIAN knows the New Testament better than he does the Old, and this is understandable. But the Bible is *one* book, and the Christian who neglects a major part of it is forfeiting rich blessings intended for his own soul. There are two good reasons why every Christian should be acquainted with the book of Joshua. First, he should know it for its historical—past and contemporary—value. The Jewish nation has never disclaimed title to the land-deed of Palestine which God gave its forefathers and which they appropriated under Joshua. From biblical prophecy and the stirrings of current events it is obvious that the most dramatic history of the land is yet to be written. Second, the book of Joshua is filled with spiritual lessons on how the Christian may live the victorious life (rest-land living) spoken of in Hebrews 3 and 4.

It is the author's wish that this brief commentary will enhance the reader's study of Joshua with the above values in view. The biblical text consistently referred to in the commentary is that of the American Standard Version. References to other versions are so designated. May the Lord magnify this portion of His inspired message.

IRVING L. JENSEN

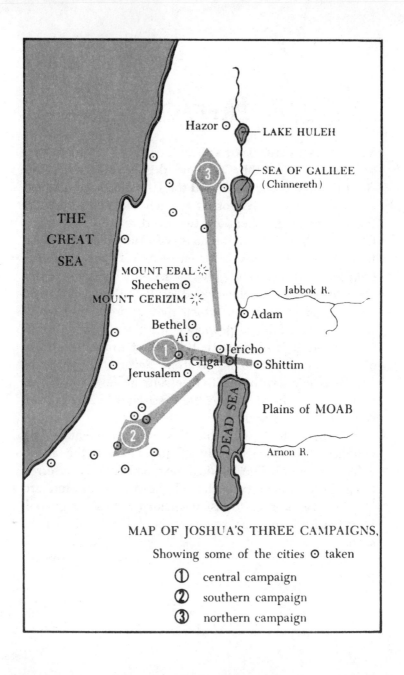

MAP OF JOSHUA'S THREE CAMPAIGNS,

Showing some of the cities ⊙ taken

① central campaign
② southern campaign
③ northern campaign

INTRODUCTION

EVEN THE CASUAL READER of the last chapter of Deuteronomy cannot help being moved by the stirring scenes described in its twelve verses: Faithful Moses sadly views from Mount Pisgah the promised land which God forbids him to enter; then, aged but not weary, he dies and is buried. The children of Israel weep for him thirty days; and his epitaph is recorded for all ages, "There arose not a prophet since in Israel like unto Moses, whom the Lord knew face to face." But the story does not end there, and as the reader instinctively glances at the next words of the holy writ, in the first verses of Joshua he finds the drama of God's people and the land renewed in a successor to Moses, and his hopes are happily stirred. This is his inspiration to study the book of Joshua; and the pursuit of it, as he applies its many precious lessons, will prove exceedingly rewarding.

Author and Date

The author of this sixth book of the Old Testament is nowhere identified in the Bible. Opinion of biblical scholars is divided as to whether or not Joshua, the main character of the book, also wrote it. However, the study

9

of the book about Joshua is not hindered by the unsettled question of its authorship.

Concerning some aspects of the book's authorship
there can be substantial assurance and agreement:

1) The author was an eyewitness of much of the historical account. The minute details and vivid descriptions of such events as the crossing of the Jordan, the
capture of Jericho, and Joshua's farewell message point
to on-the-spot observation and participation. Also, like
the "we" sections of Acts, there are a few instances of
autobiographical reporting, using the personal pronouns
(5:1[1]; 5:6; 15:4).

2) The book was written very early, not long after
the events themselves had transpired. This is indicated
by the frequent appearance of the phrase "unto this day"
and the context in which it is found. For example, Rahab,
who protected the lives of Joshua's spies, was still living
when the author wrote the book: "But Rahab . . . dwelt
in the midst of Israel unto this day" (6:25).[2]

3) Joshua is *specifically* identified as author of some
writings. He wrote the words of a covenant which he
shared with Israel "in the book of the law of God"
(24:25), which was born of his farewell charge in
chapter 24. Also Joshua was responsible for the land
survey of Canaan which he caused to have recorded in
a book (18:9).

4) Some small parts could not have been written by
Joshua. Such sections include the references to his death

----

[1]The marginal note for 5:1 (American Standard Version) reads,
"Another reading is, *they.*"
[2]Other such references are 8:28-29; 9:27; 10:27; 13:13; 14:14;
15:63 (which point to a pre-Davidic date), and 16:10 (pre-
Solomonic date).

(24:29-30) and to the faithfulness of Israel during the years after his death (24:31). It is possible that these sections were added by Eleazar the priest, and that the note of Eleazar's death (24:33) was in turn recorded by Phinehas his son.

5) The bulk of the book was written by one author. The unity of the book as to style and organization is sufficient evidence that Joshua is the composition of one man, whoever he was.

Jewish tradition, both ancient and modern, has consistently ascribed the authorship of the book to the man Joshua. Among conservative Christians today opinion is perhaps equally divided.[3] Internally, there is nothing to deny the bulk of the book to Joshua's pen. The important thing to recognize is that the identification of the author is not vital to the study of the book. For the book is a historical account of Israel's conquest and division of Canaan under the leadership of Joshua, with no *primary* autobiographical purpose of giving detailed insight into the heart of the general. If the book was of such an autobiographical purpose, identification of the author would be vital.

Place in the Old Testament

The arrangement of the thirty-nine books of the *English* Old Testament follows essentially that of the Latin

[3]Here are three representative positions by conservatives on the Joshua authorship: "Yes": Gleason L. Archer (*A Survey of Old Testament Introduction,* Chicago: Moody Press, 1964), p. 252; "No": Robert Jamieson, A. R. Fausset, and David Brown (*A Commentary on the Old and New Testaments,* Vol. II Grand Rapids: Wm. B. Eerdmans Pub. Co., (1948), p. 210; "Possibly": Merrill F. Unger (*Introductory Guide to the Old Testament,* Grand Rapids: Zondervan Pub. House, 1951), p. 281.

Vulgate (around A.D. 400) which in turn was derived
from the Greek Septuagint (third and second centuries
B.C.). The books are arranged in such an order that four
groups appear: Pentateuch, History, Poetry and Ethics,
and Prophecy. In this arrangement Joshua is the first of
the twelve historical books. The arrangement of the
Hebrew Old Testament is vastly different, though the
text content is identical. The Hebrew Old Testament
contains three groups, namely, Law, Prophets, and Writings. The Prophets section is divided into two parts,
Former and Latter. Joshua is the first book of the
Former Prophets, followed in order by Judges, Samuel
(I and II Samuel), and Kings (I and II Kings). Plac-
ing Joshua among prophetical books may have been because its author was considered to hold the office of
prophet;[4] more likely because the historical record illustrated the great principles which prophets preached.[5]

It is helpful for the student to have clear in his mind
the place the book of Joshua occupies in the historical
thread of the Old Testament books as concerns Israel.
Simply stated, the Old Testament history of Israel is of
three eras,[6] centered around a LAND (Canaan) and a
GOVERNMENT (theocracy [God as Ruler]), as shown by
the following chart:

---

[4]Merrill F. Unger, *op. cit.*, p. 279.
[5]F. F. Bruce, *The Books and the Parchments*, rev. ed. (Westwood, N.J.: Fleming H. Revell Co., 1963), p. 92.
[6]More accurately there were four eras, when one considers the
restoration period (e.g., under Nehemiah). Since this was a brief
period of revival, with hearts returning to "stone" by the time of
Malachi, the simplified 3-fold division holds.

I TO THE LAND	II IN THE LAND	III FROM THE LAND
promises of, and journey to the land and theocracy	entry into and living in, the land and theocracy	taken from the land to captivity; theocracy dissolved

The contents of the first two divisions of the Hebrew Old Testament (Pentateuch, Prophets) give a comprehensive coverage to the history of the three eras shown above:

PENTATEUCH	PROPHETS	
I (Law)	II (Former Prophets)	III (Latter Prophets)
Genesis to Deuteronomy TO the land	Joshua, Judges, I and II Samuel I and II Kings IN the land	Isaiah to Malachi FROM the land

From the foregoing it can be seen how the book of Joshua picks up the historical record after the books of the Pentateuch. In Genesis God brings Israel to birth,[7] and promises to give it the land of Canaan.[8] In Exodus He delivers His people from oppression in a foreign land, and starts them on their way to the promised land, giving them laws to live by (as recorded both in Exodus and Leviticus). Numbers records the journey of Israel through the wildernesses up to the gate of

[7]To Abraham God said, "I will make of thee a great nation" (Gen. 12:2).
[8]Gen. 12:7. God later gave further details of the promise (Gen. 15:18-21).

Canaan, while Deuteronomy describes final preparations for entering the land. At this point Joshua picks
up the story, describing the conquest of the land and
the division of its territories to the tribes of Israel. In a
real sense Joshua is the *climax* of a progressive history
as well as the *commencement* of a new experience for
Israel. Thus its historical nexus gives it a strategic place
in the Old Testament Scriptures.[9]

Broad Survey of Joshua

The best way to begin the study of Joshua is to get a
sweeping "skyscraper" view of it by reading through
the book in one sitting. Since the book is not excessive
in length (24 chapters), such a cursory survey can be
accomplished by the average reader in about two hours.[10]
The reader is urged to make this preliminary survey of
the biblical text before reading the commentary section
of this work, in order to get the feel of the book of
Joshua. The profit to the student for beginning in this
manner is inestimable.

Joshua is a book about a *land* and a *people*. The land
is an inheritance promised by God, waiting to be occupied. The people are the elect nation of God, facing
the human obstacles in the way of taking the land. The
obstacles are the occasion for battle—a holy war—designed by God to oust the heathen enemies from the

[9]A suggestion that should prove fruitful to the reader is to make
a triadic study—studying one book from each of the three eras described above, making comparisons of the broad contents. This
author has experienced much blessing in studying together Numbers, Joshua, and Jeremiah, each representing a different era.

[10]For further suggestions on making a preliminary survey of a
Bible book, see Irving L. Jensen, *Independent Bible Study* (Chicago: Moody Press, 1963), pp. 106-113.

land. The account of the book of Joshua is presented in a logical sequence of four sections, the first two of which, comprising the *action* section of the book, lead up to a peak of attaining the promised goal, as represented by a phrase of the key verse, "So Joshua took the whole land" (11:23). From this midpoint of the book the account then levels off to a plateau, as it were, to present the immediate business of Joshua, that of dividing the inheritances of land among the tribes, followed by a fitting intense appeal and exhortation to the people to fulfill the conditions for anticipated heights of continued blessing in God's rest-land. This outline of Joshua is shown in the following diagram:

STRUCTURAL OUTLINE OF JOSHUA

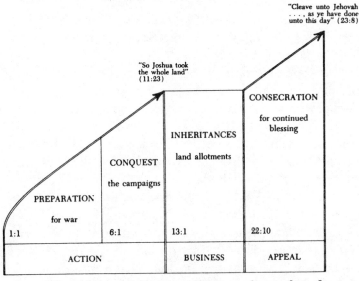

Also to be observed in the above outline of Joshua is the anticipatory character of two of the four sections:

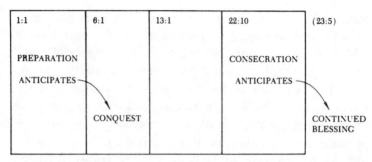

As stated earlier, the *land* of Canaan is a key particular in the account of Joshua. It is the inheritance promised, the dwelling place in which to settle down. The four sections of Joshua tell this story of the land:

| 1) entry into the land | 2) fighting for the land | 3) dividing the land | 4) living in the land |

Joshua, the key person of the book, was given this charge concerning the land: "For thou shalt cause this people to *inherit the land*" (1:6).

The book of Joshua is thus the story of rest-land won. Much attention is focused upon the *people* of the book. While Joshua is the main single character throughout (and in this real sense it is the book *of Joshua*), the spiritual lessons to be derived are learned more from the people than from Joshua. He is their leader, but their successes are generally recorded as conditional on *their* relationship to God. In the first section (*Preparation*) the charge is to *them;* the divine appointment of Joshua as their military leader is for *their* instruction; the miraculous passage through the Jordan waters is for *their* confidence; the circumcision and passover rites are for *their* preparation. In the *Conquest* section, the victories depend on *their* faith and obedience, while defeats are traced to *their* sin. In the third section (*Inheritances*), the apportionment of the lands is for *them; they* are the ones to perpetuate their tribe names in association with geographical locations. And finally, in the *Consecration* section, while the speaker throughout is the man of God who unquestionably was the individual key to the conquest of the land, the raised arm of exhortation with its finger of warning is directed to the people themselves, to assure an increasing growth in spiritual stature for their generations to come.

As suggested earlier, a fitting key verse for the book of Joshua is 11:23, a verse containing four important elements of this era of Israel's story:

1) the *conquest:* "So Joshua took the whole land"
2) the *fulfillment* of promise: "according to all that Jehovah spake unto Moses"
3) the *allotment* to the people: "and Jehovah gave it for an inheritance unto Israel according to their divisions by their tribes"
4) the *rest:* "And the land had rest from war"

The Land of Canaan

1. *Geography of the land*

The land originally promised to Abraham's seed extended from the "river of Egypt"[11] to the "great river" Euphrates (Gen. 15:18). The same promise was con-

---

[11]The "river of Egypt" is either (1) the Wadi el Arish, or "brook of Egypt" (cf. Joshua 15:4, 47), which was the boundary line between Egypt and the southern deserts of Canaan, or (2) the Nile River. In either case, the land limit is *Egypt*. It is interesting to observe that the southwestern boundary of present-day Israel is just a few miles east of the Wadi el Arish.

firmed to the Israelites in the days of Moses (Exodus 23:31), and again to Joshua (Joshua 1:4). These were the two ideal limits of influence, from the one world power on Palestine's southwestern border, Egypt, to the power on its eastern side, Babylon. One can easily recognize the strategic location of Canaan with reference to the rest of the world of Israel's day. It was the connecting link, the point of balance and the spot on which the major land and sea routes converged.[12] The explicit details of the geographical boundaries of the Canaan[13] to be possessed were described by the Lord to Moses on the eve of Israel's entry into the land (Numbers 34:1-15). At that time also Joshua and Eleazar were appointed to the task of apportioning the territories to the different tribes. The accomplishment of this business is recorded in Joshua 13—19. It is to be noted that all the enemies were not routed immediately; some cities within the boundaries were not taken until the days of David and Solomon. This piecemeal conquest can be attributed partly to the failure of the Israelites to obey fully God's conditions. Another factor was the divine timetable of designed delay, to spare the land from sudden desolation by nature itself: "I will not drive them out from before thee in one year, lest the land become desolate, and the beasts of the field multiply against thee. By little and little I will drive them out before thee, until

[12]See Denis Baly, *The Geography of the Bible* (New York: Harper and Bros. Publishers, 1957), p. 5.
[13]The name "Canaan" in the Bible, especially when used in the phrase "land of Canaan" (as in Num. 34:2), usually refers to the combined areas known today as Palestine and Syria, rather than to the smaller coastal territory of the heathen people called Canaanites. It is in this large sense that the term "Canaan" is used also in this book, unless otherwise specified.

thou be increased, and inherit the land" (Exodus 23:29-30).

The map on page 8 marks the major movements of the Israelite hosts against the enemies, which fall naturally into three general campaigns:

1) the central campaign—to secure a bridgehead for the Israelites in the center of the land, from which to spread out
2) the southern campaign—to rout the nearest foes
3) the northern campaign—to gain control of the distant territory

The map on page 112 shows an approximate identification of the boundaries of the lands allotted to the various tribes after the major campaigns were completed.

2. *Climate and resources of the land*

Because the vital factors of soil, water, weather, and climate in a particular area can change markedly over a period of a few thousand years, our knowledge of these important elements concerning the land of Canaan in Joshua's day is more accurately based on the biblical descriptions than on our present-day observations. God Himself described the land as a land of hills and valleys, blessed with rain, cared for by Himself throughout all the seasons (Deut. 11:11-12). It was a very productive land, its thirst quenched by brooks of water, fountains, and springs (Deut. 8:7); flowing with milk and honey (Exodus 3:8; 13:5; Lev. 20:24; Ezek. 20:6); abounding in wheat, barley, vines, fig trees, pomegranates, and olive trees (Deut. 8:8; II Kings 18:32); its hills offering iron and copper (Deut. 8:9). Most of the agriculture

centered in middle and north Canaan, while the plains
east of the Jordan provided excellent pasturage. The
land was also a pleasant and healthy region for dwelling,
especially because of its relatively moderate climate.
There were places where the climate was uncomfortable,
but the people could avoid these because of the topographical variety of the land. Finally, the land was
attractive for its beauty. The hills and valleys, rivers
and lakes, distant snowclad mountain peaks, green plains,
and sweeping stretches of beach afforded a lifetime experience of exulting in the marvelous handiwork of God.

God was giving the *best* to His people!

3. *History of the land*

When Abraham first arrived in Canaan from his homeland of Chaldea, the land, within Egypt's sphere of influence, was spottily inhabited by nomadic and semi-
nomadic tribes.[14] The names of some of these tribes are
recorded in Genesis: Perizzites, Amorites, Philistines,
Hittites, and so on (see Gen. 14:5-7; 15:19-21). Now,
hundreds of years later as Joshua reached the land, the
situation was different mainly in this respect: The small
nomadic tribes had now grown to the proportion of
populated city-states, centered about fortified cities. The
enemy which Israel faced was not one unified nation.[15]
Rather, it was a battery of scattered peoples (Hittites,

[14]K. A. Kitchen says, "It is certain that Canaanites and Amorites
were well established in Syria-Palestine by 2000 B.C." See "Canaan," *The New Bible Dictionary* (Grand Rapids: Wm. B. Eerdmans Pub. Co., 1962), p. 184. For an up-to-date treatment of this
subject, see Howard F. Vos, *Genesis and Archaeology* (Chicago:
Moody Press, 1963), pp. 85-91.

[15]The record of Joshua, for example, does not indicate that Israel had to contend with the nation of Egypt to take Canaan.

Hivites, Amorites, etc.), a situation demanding the strategy of individual battles for the most part, but demanding also the ability to strike at any coalition of such heathen powers.

The Man Joshua

1. *His Name*

Joshua, son of Nun, of the tribe of Ephraim, was originally named Hoshea (Num. 13:8), which means literally "salvation." At some time during the wilderness journey (Num. 13:16) Moses changed the name to Yehoshua (Jehoshua), which is printed in our Bibles in the contracted form of Joshua. Jehoshua, or Joshua, means literally "Jehovah is salvation."[16] Moses' choice of this name reflects the spiritual qualities which he must have seen in his attendant Joshua, and also reveals the sacredness which he identified with Joshua's ministry, aware that his own mantle of service to God would very likely be transferred to his understudy at his decease.

2. *His Career*

Joshua was born in Egypt and experienced the extreme oppression heaped upon his brethren by Pharaoh. He was a young man at the time of Israel's exodus from that foreign land (Exodus 33:11), and must have early displayed to Moses his faith in God and a devoted spirit of service. The fact that his grandfather Elishama was captain and head of the tribe of Ephraim (Num. 1:10;

[16]Other Old Testament names constructed like Jehoshua are Jehoiakim ("Jehovah exalteth"), Jehohanan ("Jehovah is gracious"), and Elisha ("God is deliverance"). It is interesting also to note that the Greek spelling of the Hebrew name Jehoshua is "Jesus." The name "Jesus" in Hebrews 4:8 (A.V.) is really Joshua.

2:18) no doubt helped to bring Joshua to the attention of Moses, and subsequently he was appointed Moses' minister.

a. *as attendant of Moses*

Throughout the wilderness journeys Joshua stood at the side of Moses, ministering to him in the herculean task of leading two million people on their treacherous march to Canaan. Only a few of the special tasks he fulfilled are recorded in the Bible. At Rephidim Moses appointed him to repel the attack of the formidable Amalekites, which task was accomplished in a day (Exodus 17:8-16). At Sinai Moses chose Joshua to accompany him to the mount on the occasion of receiving the law and the commandment (Exodus 24:12-13). From the wilderness of Paran Moses sent Joshua with eleven others to spy out the land of Canaan in anticipation of the forthcoming military engagements between Israel and the enemies in the land (Num. 13:1-16). Joshua and Caleb alone had the faith to believe that Israel could conquer the enemy with God's help, in the face of the human odds against them. This was the crucial test of Joshua's young life, and it determined his career thereafter. Had he joined the other ten in their negative report, he would have reaped the judgment of immediate death by plague (Num. 14:36-37). For standing alone with Caleb, Joshua was granted the privilege of later entering the land of Canaan (Num. 14:26-35). On him also fell the awesome responsibility of *leading* the younger generation of Israelites into that land.

b. *as successor to Moses*

When Moses knew that for a past sin he had forfeited

the privilege of leading his people into Canaan, and that he would die before they made that entrance, he asked God to name his successor, so that his people would not be as "sheep which have no shepherd" (Num. 27:17). God's choice was Joshua, whom He described as "a man in whom is the Spirit" (Num. 27:18). Moses surely must have been moved with gratitude to God to know that his own leadership would be perpetuated in a very real sense in the service of the one whom he had trained along the way. And Moses "laid his hands upon him [Joshua]: and the children of Israel hearkened unto him" (Deut. 34:9).

Joshua could not hope to be another Moses. Moses was unique among the prophets of God in the sense of how much was accomplished through him to the glory of God (cf. Deut. 34:10-12). But Joshua's experiences in many ways paralleled those of Moses. Both were given charges to serve in leadership (Moses at Horeb, Joshua at Jericho); both led Israel bodily from one land to another (Moses, from Egypt; Joshua, into Canaan); both experienced the miracle of the parting of the waters (Moses, the Red Sea; Joshua, the Jordan River); both gave moving farewell addresses (Moses at Moab,[17] Joshua at Shechem[18]); and when each died the people of Israel were at a peak of spiritual health, determined to serve the Lord.[19]

---

[17]Deuteronomy 31:30–33:29.
[18]Joshua 23:1–24:28.
[19]At Moses' death, Israel continued to obey God's commands through Joshua, "and did as Jehovah commanded Moses" (Deut. 34:9). At Joshua's death, the last significant words of Israel were "Jehovah our God will we serve, and unto his voice will we hearken" (Joshua 24:24).

3. *His Character*

No greater commendation of Joshua's character was made than that made by God: "a man in whom is the Spirit," that is, Joshua was filled with the Spirit (Num. 27:18; cf. Deut. 34:9). This determined everything else that he was. He feared God utterly, so that he expected Israel to be consumed whenever sin was harbored in the camp. His faith was deep, strong, pure, and enduring—a vital quality in making him the courageous general that he was, undaunted by impossible things. The spirit of obedience which he learned as a devoted follower of Moses was that which he rendered his Commander-in-chief, God, in the mighty tasks given him in Canaan. He was a great ruler, commanding the respect of all his subjects (Deut. 34:9), maintaining order and discipline, putting the worship of God central in the nation's government, encouraging his people to press on to claim God's best. He was also a great military leader, using his God-given traits of wisdom, confidence, courage, and a spirit of challenge to manipulate his army in strategies that consistently led to triumph.

And last but not least, Joshua was a humble man who thought highly of others and most gloriously of God. Such a man God was pleased to use.

Applying the Message of Joshua Today

Like the other historical books of the Old Testament, Joshua has much to say about who God is, and what man is like, with emphasis on the former. God is shown to be holy, almighty, sovereign, just, full of mercy, a designer of order, worthy of worship, and a rewarder of those who fear and obey Him. These and other truths of the character and works of God are profusely illustrated throughout the book of Joshua.

What makes Joshua so practical for the Christian is that its major application concerns the Christian's pursuit of that abundant life which Christ talked about when He said, "I have come for people to have life and have it till it overflows" (John 10:10, Charles B. Williams translation). Israel dwelling in the rest-land of Canaan is a vivid type of the Christian living in intimate relationship to Christ, abiding in Him (John 15:4), and being filled with His joy (John 15:11). The Christian's rest is a peace that comes out of victory over the soul's enemies, through the power and help of God (Heb. 4:9-10).

The story of Joshua is the story of God's people driving the enemies out of Canaan, so that they might take the promised land inheritance, and make their dwelling place there. The Israelites were *promised* all the land, but would *possess* only what they would appropriate and receive from God. This Joshua made very clear when he said to the people, "*Go in* to possess the land, which Jehovah your God giveth you" (Joshua 1:11). For the Christian, the blessings of abiding in Christ originate in the divine act of regeneration, but are contingent upon the Christian's diligence to enter into that abiding life (Heb. 4:11).

But the foes of Israel were many and formidable. Whether it was a flooded river to cross, a strong fortress to destroy, or an alliance of armies to conquer, the entrance and possession were impossible—without God. But God was with Israel, and God fought for Israel, and this made the difference. How very vital for the

Christian intent on having God's best to learn that the
enemies (so many!) of his soul are not driven out by
his impotent efforts, well intended as they may be, but
by God's devastating dynamite; not by the arm of flesh,
but by the whole armor of God (Eph. 6).

When Israel's major campaigns were over, the newly
gained land was divided among the tribes. Now it was
the Israelites' task to maintain and multiply the blessings
of dwelling in the place given by God. It was no easy
task, but the Israelites were enlightened as to how to
accomplish it: in the same manner by which they secured
the land in the first place. Thus the reader of Joshua
will see on every page illustrations of God's conditions
for the Christian's securing, maintaining, and multiply-
ing the blessings of the rest promised by Jesus, "Ye shall
find rest unto your souls" (Matt. 11:29).

Purposes of the Commentary

Basically, this commentary is intended to throw a spot-
light on the great movements of the book of Joshua and
to show how the story describes one vital experience of
God's people. Besides furnishing introductory background material for the study of Joshua, the author has
also attempted to elucidate obscure or difficult portions
of the biblical text, which accounts for many of the
footnotes. The ultimate purpose of the commentary is
to encourage the reader's further study in Joshua, to
derive many more fruitful lessons in his own personal
experience of victoriously abiding in Christ.

PART ONE

PREPARATION FOR THE CONQUEST
(1:1—5:15)

I. INITIAL ORDERS (1:1—2:24)
   A. The Mobilization (1:1-18)
   B. The Reconnaissance (2:1-24)

II. MILITARY PREPARATION (3:1—5:1)
   A. Tactical Positioning
   B. Recognition of Leadership (3:1—4:18)
   C. Recognition of Strength (4:19—5:1)

III. SPIRITUAL PREPARATION (5:2-15)
   A. The Token of Circumcision (5:2-9)
   B. The Token of Blood (5:10)
   C. The Token of Fruit (5:11-12)
   D. The Token of a Sword (5:13-15)

Part One

PREPARATION FOR THE CONQUEST

(1:1–5:15)

I. INITIAL ORDERS (1:1–2:24)

THE JOURNEY from Egypt to Canaan, described in the earlier books of the Old Testament, has now reached its final stage. The multitudes of Israelites are encamped on the eastern side of the Jordan, on the plains of Moab just north of the Dead Sea. Since the day of God's command to Pharaoh, "Let my people go," the expedition of the Israelites has demonstrated very visibly that this is no project of human design: the directions came originally from God; the daily sustenance was supernatural; the obstacles were overcome by miraculous help; and discipline was meted out by divine wisdom. Now, for the unfinished task, a new day sets in motion the communication of the chain of command: God speaks to Joshua (1:1-9); Joshua commands his officers (1:10-11a; 2:1); the officers in turn command the people (1:11-18). This is the day for the initial orders of the holy war of occupation.

A. The Mobilization (1:1-18)

1. *Charge to the Commander* (1:1-9)

When the thirty days' mourning over Moses' death had
come to an end (Deut. 34:8), and when all the tears of
deep grief (no professional mourning here!) over the
departure of this man of God had cleansed the spiritual
eyes to see more clearly from the perspective of the eter-
nities, God spoke from heaven directly to Joshua and
reiterated his appointment as successor to Moses which
had been given him earlier by Moses.[1] The work of God
must go on. His servants die, but God does not die, no
less His divine program. "Moses my servant is dead,"
God said to Joshua; "now, therefore . . . thou . . ." (1:2).
Joshua was now sovereignly appointed as the man of the
hour, but he was not to forget the one he was succeeding.
God reminded him of three important truths concerning
Moses' experience: first, that to Moses was spoken God's
promise of the land (1:3); second, that God was with
Moses in his ministry of leadership (1:5); and third, that
the law of God delivered by Moses was to continue as the
people's law of life (1:7). These vital reminders to Joshua
were certainly to serve him often in the arduous and try-
ing years to come as he would reminisce about his service
to his human master Moses and about this day of divine
appointment.

But as noted earlier in the Introduction, while this book
of the Bible is about the man Joshua, it is primarily about
the people of God. In the commission to Joshua, God
used the term "thou"—as successor to Moses— but also
"and all this people . . . even . . . the children of Israel"

[1]See Numbers 27:15-23.

(1:2).[2] Each individual Israelite was a soul loved by his Maker and Lord, and there was a beautiful dwelling-lot awaiting him in the land of inheritance. He, with Joshua his leader, was commanded to arise, cross the Jordan, and claim the land (1:2). This was the extent of the commission in its most general terms.

Next God spoke in more detail about the land to be occupied (1:3-4). The extent of it was enormous.[3] From the description one can visualize Joshua as standing facing the west, hearing God describe the boundaries. To Joshua's left was the distant southern boundary, "the wilderness," or "desert," the region west and south of the Dead Sea which formed a natural boundary between Canaan and the Sinai Peninsula. Then Joshua's eyes were turned to the distant peaks of the northern limits, "this Lebanon," the mountain range far north-northwest of the Sea of Galilee. Behind Joshua, to the east, lay the eastern boundary, the Euphrates;[4] while in the direction of the setting sun, under the skyline of the Judean hills, spread the western limit, "the great sea." In between the four extremities described was Canaan itself, here represented by one of the major peoples then occupying it, the Hittites. This was the land offered by God. The com-

[2]At only one other place in this commission are the Israelites referred to explicitly (v. 6). But the spirit and principles of the commission unquestionably apply to the nation, as Joshua is charged to lead them.

[3]A study of the passages in the Bible where the land promise is recorded fails to indicate that the one to whom the promise was related (whether Abraham, Moses, or Joshua) had any questions about the details of the geographical boundaries. Whatever the description, the impact of enormity was surely transmitted; the hearer evidently was content to let history write out the boundaries in due course of time.

[4]It was not until the reigns of David and Solomon that Israel's dominion reached this far east.

mand was to occupy *all* of it, not just to register a theo-
retical claim to it.

But there were enemies in the land to be occupied,
and their expulsion was the subject of God's next words
to Joshua (1:5-6). A lifetime of continuous victory over
all enemies was assured Joshua (and therefore the people) through faith and courage on the basis of the unfailing presence and miraculous help of God: "I will be
with thee; I will not fail thee, nor forsake thee" (1:5).
The success and prosperity which God promised had
their source therefore in God Himself. Without God,
there would be defeat; with God, success. But woven
into the sovereign design of success for Joshua and the
people was the human strand of the condition of their
obedience: "Only be strong . . . to observe to *do* according to all the law" (1:7). They were to magnify the
Word by their lips, and edify their souls by continually
meditating on its precepts. Then *doing* according to the
law would be the inevitable fruit.

The enemies in the land? "Be not affrighted, neither
be thou dismayed: for Jehovah thy God is with thee
whithersoever thou goest" (1:9).

                              *   *   *

The charge to Joshua is filled with lessons for Christians on enjoying spiritual success and prosperity. Successful living is a promise of God, a gift of God, attain-
able by the help of God. Its potentialities are enormous,
waiting only to be appropriated. Enemies of the soul—
Satan, the world, and the flesh—need to be driven out,
but they are enemies of God, and so He promises all the
help needed for conquering them. The condition laid
to the Christian is costly but absolutely necessary: living

in constant obedience in the light of God's Word. The blessings of victorious living come by *invitation* to the Christian, but the conditions for its fulfillment come by *mandate*. Christians, like Joshua, cannot escape the divine words loud and clear: "Have not I *commanded* thee?" (1:9).

2. *Charge to the People* (1:10-18)

Jehovah God, Commander-in-chief of Israel, began His war against the Canaanites by charging Joshua to lead the people into the land. Down through the levels of command, the orders were delivered to bring a host of two million people[5] to their feet to find their places in the complex military strategy of such a vast campaign. The reader of the book of Joshua must continually prod his imagination to visualize the awesome task of General Joshua to lead such a large host of people into the land. The fact that the large size of the Israelite band is not made a prominent factor in the record of the book of Joshua speaks well for the orderliness and discipline with which Joshua maneuvered the hosts. In strict military fashion, reflecting the training he had received under Moses, Joshua delegated the officers under him to mobilize the people to the state of readiness. In a sense they had always been ready, because they knew the journey was not over. But the rigors of the Transjordan campaign demanded a time of respite in camp, which

[5]The number of Israelite male warriors reaching the plains of Moab was 601,730 (Num. 26:51). Assuming the number of all other males to be approximately the same, and the total number of females to equal the total number of males, the total population must have been approximately two million. See Irving L. Jensen, *Numbers*. (Chicago: Moody Press, 1964), pp. 16-17, 107-108.

they were afforded. Now they must prepare to move,
which involved provisions, tents, cattle, and the gathering of fruit and grain from the fields of the plain.[6] The
key word of Joshua's order to the people was *prepare*.
Joshua anticipated that the Israelites would be crossing
the Jordan within three days, though as it turned out,
the extended trip of the spies (chap. 2) apparently de-
layed the crossing by at least three days.[7]

Joshua's second order of business in mobilizing the
troops for action concerned the special group comprising
the tribes of Reuben and Gad and the half-tribe of
Manasseh (1:12-18). The key word delivered to them
was *remember*. They had earlier agreed, in return for
being allotted the rich pastureland of Transjordan, to
help their brethren possess the land west of the Jordan
before settling down in their own territories (Num. 32).
Now Joshua brought to their remembrance this promise
they had made, and called for the mobilization of their
"mighty men of valor," an army of about 40,000.[8] Their
reply was enthusiastic, and revealed all the elements of
a spirit of devotion and cooperation (1:16-18):

1) *obedience:* "we will do," "we will go," "we will
   hearken"

[6]Daily manna was still being given them at this time; but they
were not forbidden to eat of the fruit of Moab. Besides, their cattle needed to be cared for.
[7]Cf. 1:11, 2:22, and 3:2.
[8]Cf. Joshua 4:13. The recent census of these two and one-half
tribes disclosed there were 110,000 male warriors. Joshua's call
for "*all* the mighty men of valor" must not be interpreted as
though Joshua was calling for all of the 110,000 men, for (1) the
protection of the women, children, and cattle demanded a guard,
and (2) mere numbers of warriors do not determine victory.
Joshua's battle plans obviously demanded only the 40,000.

2) *faith* and *hope:* "only Jehovah thy God be with thee" (they knew there would be no victory without God)

3) *intolerance of sin:* "he . . . that shall rebel . . . shall be put to death"

4) *support by encouragement:* "be [thou] strong and of good courage"

B. The Reconnaissance (2:1-24)

Joshua had utter confidence in God to lead Israel to victory, as shown in his charge to the people. But this did not mean a laying down of arms to watch God work. The plans of military strategy, the calculated risk of casualties, and the bloody clashes of battle were all to be part of the projected campaigns of conquest. To spy the land before launching the attack was not to doubt God; it was to fulfill the obligation of wise military strategy as to the *manner* and *course* of battle, and then commit the outcome to God.

The most obvious feature of this intriguing chapter is the fact that while it is an account about the mission of two young spies, a woman by the name of Rahab is the main character throughout most of its verses (vv. 2-22). How the story of Rahab is woven into the main plot about the spies is shown in the following double outline for the chapter:

THE SPIES	VERSES	RAHAB
1. Spies are dispatched	1	
2. Spies are protected	2-7	Rahab's works
3. Spies are informed	8-11	Rahab's faith
4. Spies promise safety	12-22	Rahab's reward
5. Spies give report	23-24	

The key paragraph is 2:8-11 because this vital informa-
tion given to the spies by Rahab constituted the essence
of their report to Joshua.

The place of Rahab in the history of Israel was twofold. *First,* she was chosen by God to provide the in-
formation which He desired Israel to have at this time,
namely, that He had melted the hearts of the enemy in
fear of Joshua and his hosts, even as Moses had proph-
esied earlier (Exodus 15:13-18). *Second,* Rahab would
be for all centuries to come a vivid example of the sin-
ner, through whom God accomplishes His purposes and
in whose heart He works a change. Concerning this
latter, it is to be observed that a harlot[9] is Israel's helper.
Rahab the harlot is cited in the genealogical record of
Jesus (Matt. 1:5); and James and the author of Hebrews
commend her for her works and faith (James 2:25;
Heb. 11:31).

1. *The Spies Are Dispatched* (2:1)

The people were camping in the area known as Shit-
tim[10] when Joshua secretly dispatched the two young[11]
men to spy out the land on the other side of the Jordan,
particularly in the area of Jericho. The reconnaissance
project was apparently kept secret from the Israelites,

[9]Some feel that the word translated "harlot" was the official
designation of the woman of the lodging house, without in itself
designating whether she was an innkeeper or a "pleasure-woman"
(Berkeley Version, footnote). But it is to be observed that the
phrase "Rahab the harlot" appears also in two instances in the
New Testament (Heb. 11:31; James 2:25), where the designation
of Rahab's profession seems to be emphasized for a special reason.

[10]Shittim was located in the foothills of the eastern edge of the
Jordan Valley, off the northeast corner of the Dead Sea. The distance from it to Jericho was about fourteen miles, with the Jordan
dividing the distance equally.

[11]Cf. 6:23.

very likely because Joshua wanted to avoid a repetition
of the disastrous sequel to the majority report to Moses
of the twelve spies (of which he was one of the minority
of two) about forty years previously. That only two spies
were sent indicates that the reconnaissance was obviously
only for the immediate vicinity of the fortress at Jericho,
which did not call for a large expedition. No doubt also
the two men Joshua chose were men of strong faith like
himself and Caleb, who would turn in an affirmative
recommendation for attack despite human odds against
them. For the object of the spies' mission was to determine not *whether* but *when* and *how* an attack should
be made. Joshua's training in the wilderness was paying
off every day.

Joshua's special interest in Jericho reveals his wisdom
as a military strategist. A study of a topographical map
of Canaan discloses the excellent location of Jericho as
a bridgehead for all subsequent advances to the west,
south, and north. Jericho was located on a large fertile
plain at the foot of the Judean hills and at the entrance
to one of their passageways. Here also was ample camping ground for the nonmilitary Israelite hosts while the
warriors were off to battle. To the general of the army
of Israel, the conquest of Canaan depended on gaining
the bridgehead of Jericho.

2. *The Spies Are Protected* (2:2-7)

The spies could not conceal their identity as Israelites
as they walked the streets of Jericho, mixing with the
people and posing as their brethren. They found a lodging place for the night in the house of Rahab, unaware
that they had already been spotted as spies. The in-

formed king of Jericho sent men to Rahab's house to apprehend them, but believing Rahab's subtle lie that the spies had already left, the king's men continued their pursuit outside the city's gate, while Joshua's men hid safely on Rahab's roof, under stalks of flax.

There can be no question but that Rahab lied. Her lie was the protection of the spies. Did therefore the end (protection) justify the means (lying)? The answer must be negative, since lying is always sin, and sin is never justified by God. Rahab's actions must be interpreted in light of the total picture. First, one must believe that God could have protected the spies without Rahab's lie. Further, the commendation of Rahab's words in James 2:25 is not commendation of the lie which she adopted in the weakness of her flesh (and not beyond the scope of God's forgiveness), but of the selfless act of doing something to help God's cause in defiance of her own national ties.[12]

3. *The Spies Are Informed* (2:8-11)

Before the spies went to sleep, Rahab opened her heart to them, and revealed the reason for her protection of their lives. What she said to the spies would document their report and recommendation to Joshua concerning the Canaanites. Rahab was emphatic in her disclosures:

1) *her own conclusion:* that the Israelites would take Canaan by the help of their Lord: "I know that Jehovah hath given you the land" (2:9).
2) *her people's defeatism:* that the Canaanites were fearful and benumbed after hearing the report of

---

[12]Compare also the actions of the Hebrew midwives (Exodus 1:17 ff.) and the woman at Bahurim (II Sam. 17:18-20).

God's drying up the Red Sea and Israel's slaughter
of the Amorites (2:10).

3) *her own faith:* this was faith in seed stage, identifying Israel's Lord as God over all—heaven above,
and earth beneath (2:11).

4. *The Spies Promise Safety* (2:12-22)

In return for Rahab's sparing their lives, the spies
gratefully consented to her request for protection. Rahab
and the other members of her father's household would
be spared death in the day of Israel's assault on Jericho
on three conditions: (1) they should remain in the house
during the assault (2:19)—the very house which was the
haven for the spies; (2) a cord of scarlet thread or yarn
should hang from the very window through which the
spies were let down by a strong rope (2:18); and (3) the
mission of the spies must be kept secret (2:20). On
Rahab's acceptance of the conditions, the spies departed
into the wilds of the nearby mountain,[13] while she lost
no time in binding the scarlet thread in the window,
sealing her deliverance. What a beautiful picture of the
believer's salvation, very much like the earlier experience
of the Israelites in Egypt, when God said to them, "When
I see the blood, I will pass over you" (Exodus 12:13).
When Joshua's army saw the scarlet thread, they would
spare the lives of all in the house.[14]

[13]This very likely was the mountain region of limestone cliffs and
caves south of Jericho and off the northwest corner of the Dead
Sea, well suited for hiding. (It was in the caves of this vicinity
that the Dead Sea scrolls were later hid, to be found twenty centuries after.)
[14]Some Bible students see in the scarlet thread a symbol of the
redemptive blood of Christ (cf. footnote, Berkeley Version). A
very clear illustration of salvation in this story is the deliverance
for those being found "in the house" (2:19).

5. *The Spies Report* (2:23-24)

Having eluded the pursuers from Jericho, Joshua's
spies after three days' hiding left the mountain area,
crossed the deep, flooded Jordan—obviously by swim-
ming—and returned to Joshua in the night to recount
all that had befallen them. Their own personal experiences were merely the background to the main report
they delivered to Joshua. That report is concisely recorded in the last verse of chapter 2: "Truly Jehovah
hath delivered into our hands all the land; and moreover
all the inhabitants of the land do melt away before us"
(2:24). One can sense the thrill of expectancy of victory
that surged through Joshua to hear such news. Whether
he slept through the rest of the night or used the hours
for last-minute preparations, he was up early in the
morning, organizing the hosts of Israel for the assault on
Jericho (3:1).

An important lesson for Christian living derived from
this chapter of Joshua concerns the Christian's *knowing
the enemy.* Trust in God's help for Christlike living does
not preclude being forewarned of the tactics of Satan
and being alert to this one who goes about seeking whom
he may devour, as he works through such destroyers as
lust, pride, disobedience, doubt, discouragement, and
neglect. Just as the demons despaired in the presence
of Jesus, enemies which need to be driven from the
Christian's life will melt for fear, and thus be conquerable, when they see God as *Lord of the Christian's heart*
leading His child to victory by faith. It behooves the
Christian thus to live *daily* following God his Lord.

II. MILITARY PREPARATION (3:1–5:1)

Ever since leaving Egypt, the Israelites had not been required of God to take the initiative to *reach* the land of Canaan. They simply followed the pillar of cloud. Now, to *possess* the land they must take the initiative to drive out the idolatrous nations already inhabiting it. So the offensive was now theirs. The Canaanites were waiting—though with melting hearts of fear—for the arrival of the conqueror. It was Joshua's task, as general of the army, to bring his hosts into tactical position for the first clash, identify their leadership, and measure their might. This was the military aspect of the Israelites' preparation for battles to come.

A. Tactical Positioning

Joshua's objective was to gain the bridgehead of the fortress and plain of Jericho from which he could then launch all subsequent assaults westward, southward, and northward. It was basically a strategy of position, and he must have felt himself very fortunate to have such a tactically blessed location as his first objective—not to speak of the fact that he now knew its people had, in spirit, already given up.

Before the hour of his siege against Jericho, Joshua encountered two major tasks: (1) crossing the Jordan and (2) encamping near Jericho. For the encampment, Joshua chose a plain on the eastern side of Jericho (4:19) which was to be later named Gilgal (5:9b). The crossing of the Jordan presented the major problems, some of which were:

1) The Jordan River was in its flood stage (3:15b) in the month of April during the grain harvest season. At

such a time there was no possibility of wading across the otherwise shallow ford opposite Jericho.

2) The number of the hosts of Israelites was legion. To funnel across, at one spot, two million people with cattle and possessions was not only unimaginable but unwise, militarily speaking.

3) The crossing should be completed in the daylight hours of one day.

The three days of encampment along the shores of the Jordan (3:1-2) provided the time necessary for final preparations on the eve of battle, and it was during this time that Joshua was given assurance that *somehow,* through wonders of God, his people would be able to pass over: "Tomorrow Jehovah will do wonders among you" (3:5). God apparently withheld the details of the miraculous crossing until the morning of the crossing itself (3:7).

A survey of Joshua 3 and 4 reveals the underlying intent of the historical record of Israel's movements at this time. The following chart will be helpful in understanding the basic organization—somewhat hidden—of these two chapters:

JOSHUA 3:1–5:1

3:1 3:17	4:1 4:14	4:15 4:18	4:19 5:1
CROSSING THE JORDAN			ENCAMPING AT GILGAL
PEOPLE	TWELVE LEADERS	PRIESTS	ALL
LEADERSHIP PROMINENT HERE			STRENGTH PROMINENT HERE

Geographically, the account is made up of two parts: crossing the Jordan, and encamping at Gilgal. In the section of the crossing, the *main* characters of each of the three parts are (1) the people, (2) the twelve leaders, (3) the priests.

When the chronological sequence[15] of the narrative of the Jordan crossing is sought in this section of Joshua (3:1—4:18), the order of action is the following:

1) On the day before the crossing, the people were instructed (a) as to their spiritual preparation: to sanctify themselves (3:5); (b) as to the march: to keep a distance of 2,000 cubits (3,000 feet) from the ark, following the ark as they began to see the priests bearing it (3:3-4).

2) On the morning of the crossing Jehovah gave instructions to Joshua concerning the details of the crossing. Joshua instructed the priests, the twelve leaders, and the people of their duties for the day (3:8-13).

3) March toward the river began (3:14). Joshua and the twelve leaders apparently followed immediately after the priests; then the people.

4) Priests bearing the ark reached the swollen river line and dipped their feet into the water at its edge, at which instant the river began to drop, being miraculously held back "in one head" upstream at Adam,[16] a city

[15]The section 3:1—4:18 (crossing the Jordan) was composed by the biblical author in a manner often found in Hebrew biblical history, similar to that of the flood and creation narratives. The pattern is first to recount the story to its completion, in general form, and then to backtrack chronologically, to amplify parts of the narrative without grammatically indicating such a backtrack. The continuity of this section is preserved when one reads 4:1 and 4:15 respectively thus: "And it came to pass . . . that Jehovah . . . [*had spoken*] unto Joshua, saying . . ." (cf. 3:12); "And Jehovah . . . [*had spoken*] unto Joshua, saying. . . ."

[16]The reading of the Berkeley Version of 3:16 suggests the possibility that the wall or dam of water extended from the place of the crossing to Adam.

sixteen to twenty miles north of the Jericho ford (3:16).

5) The riverbanks and bed drained of the flow of water, and the ground under the feet of the priests (who had advanced from the water's edge toward the midst of the river) dried at least to firmness. The Israelites, led by Joshua and the twelve men, now walked over quickly[17] on firm ground, "until all the nation were passed clean over the Jordan" (3:16-17). The two and a half tribes of Reuben, Gad, and Manasseh (including 40,000 warriors) were among the hosts (4:12-13).

6) The twelve men representing the twelve tribes each lifted a heavy stone from the river's bed where the priests were standing, to be eventually set up as a memorial at Gilgal (4:1-8, 20).

7) Joshua then set up a memorial of twelve stones in the Jordan at the spot where the priests were standing (4:9).[18]

8) At Joshua's signal, the priests bearing the ark left their spot in the Jordan bed and joined the Israelites on the western shore of the river. At this moment, "the waters of the Jordan returned unto their place, and went over all its banks, as aforetime" (4:18).

B. Recognition of Leadership (3:1—4:18)

While it is true that the Isralites were given a visible

[17]Cf. 4:10. The haste was to accomplish the crossing before dark. "This could easily have been accomplished in half a day, if the people formed a procession of a mile or upwards in breadth." C. F. Keil and F. Delitzsch, *Joshua, Judges, Ruth* (Grand Rapids: Wm. B. Eerdmans Pub. Co., 1950), p. 47.

[18]It was fitting that a memorial be placed at the location of the deliverance, in addition to the one to be set up at camp.

demonstration of the omnipotence of God by this miraculous parting of the Jordan, even as the Red Sea had been parted for their ancestors, the first lesson they were taught was that of leadership—for there would have been no miracle if first they had not obeyed in following the ark. The predominant lesson of 3:1—4:18 is that of leadership. Triumphant possession of Canaan demanded Israel's unceasing devotion to two leaders: God, the divine Commander, and Joshua, God's appointed general. It was vital that the divine leadership be identified and impressed upon the people at the commencement of the campaign.

1. *Divine Leadership*

The ark of the covenant of Jehovah was the visible symbol which God used at this time to direct the Israelites' eyes to His leadership. The ark, by symbol, was Jehovah. The *Wycliffe Bible Commentary* suggests this literal rendering of 3:11: "Behold the ark of the covenant! The Lord (*'adon*) of all the earth is about to proceed before you into the Jordan."[19] It was really Jehovah—not Joshua or priests or other leaders—who was at the lead of the nation. "When ye see the ark . . . go after it" (3:3). The ark would show the way over an uncharted course: "that ye may know the way by which ye must go; for ye have not passed this way heretofore" (3:4). Further, the presence of the ark would miraculously touch off the awe-inspiring sight of a river suddenly parted. The ark was the key to the miracle. This fact is first shown in the account by the oft-repeated

[19]John Rea, "Joshua," *The Wycliffe Bible Commentary* (Chicago: Moody Press, 1962), p. 210.

phrase "priests that bear the ark" (3:8, 13, 14, 15, 17) and its relation to the event. The clearest evidence, however, is explicitly given in Joshua's words in connection with the stones of memorial which were to be later set up at Gilgal: "Because the waters of the Jordan were cut off before the ark of the covenant of Jehovah: *when it passed over the Jordan, the waters of the Jordan were cut off*" (4:7).

The divine leadership was impressed on the people in another way. This came by way of the command of preparation, "Sanctify yourselves." Military preparation—men, arms, food, water—was one thing. Spiritual preparation to follow Jehovah as Commander-in-chief was another. For this, the people must sanctify themselves. Joshua was not calling for ablutions for the body, nor washings of the clothes. This was a command to examine the soul, to confess sin, and to be in right relationship to the One who was going to lead to victory.

2. *Human Leadership*

As God was with Moses, so would He be with Joshua. This was the essence of God's appointment of Joshua to succeed Moses. Now had come the time to demonstrate visibly and impress indelibly upon the hearts of the people that Joshua was their leader in behalf of God. Joshua's leading them through a miraculously parted river would be the first of his credentials for the days and years to follow. This is what God said on the morning of the crossover: "This day will I *begin* to magnify thee in the sight of all Israel, that they may know that, as I was with Moses, so I will be with thee" (3:7). That the people reacted favorably is shown by the record written after the event was over: "On that day Jehovah magnified Joshua in the sight of all Israel; and they feared him, as they feared Moses, all the days of his life" (4:14).

C. Recognition of Strength (4:19–5:1)

In the midst of the awesome spectacle of the raging torrent subdued and parted *for them,* the Israelites were given the immediate impression of God *before them* (cf. 3:11). Now, having followed their leaders to the land of Canaan, their minds were stirred to reflect more intently on the *strength* of the One who led them thus, and who would continue to lead. This accounts for the added emphasis of Joshua's interpretation of the meaning of the stones of memorial which he had set up at Gilgal (4:19-24). Earlier, he had attached the significance of *leadership* (4:6-7). Now, he exalts the *might* of God, a truth of ageless significance that should bolster Israel's confidence in the present task, and, conversely, intimidate her enemy: "For Jehovah your God dried up the waters of the Jordan . . . that all the peoples of the earth may know the hand of Jehovah, *that it is mighty;* that ye may fear Jehovah your God for ever" (4:23-24).

The miracle of the Jordan crossing left no possible suggestion of mere coincidence or favorable chance. This is confirmed by the reactions of the enemies of the land, whose hearts melted in fear when the report reached them that "Jehovah had dried up the waters of the Jordan" (5:1). Actually, the Jordan miracle was a supernatural creation of a complex of many factors:

1) the fulfillment of the foretelling of the event (3:13-14)

2) the exact timing of the event—the priests dipping their feet (3:15)

3) the rising up "in one heap" of a wall of water[20] (3:16)

4) the fact that this happened at flood stage (3:15)

5) whatever was the retaining power or "wall," it had to hold back the onrushing Jordan north of the spot, including all its tributaries, throughout most of a day

6) in very short time the drained soft river bottom became firm as "dry ground" (3:17)

7) the timing of the returning flow of the Jordan, as the priests with the ark left the river bottom (4:18)

The might of their Leader was the message of the day, as the hosts of Israel encamped on the east border of Jericho[21] on the tenth day of the first month, very appropriately on the fortieth anniversary of the preparation of the paschal lamb which anticipated the exodus from Egypt (Exodus 12:3).

The Christian's quest for the secret of victorious living is aided much by the experience of Israel crossing the Jordan. The major obstacle of the Christian's entrance into the rest-land of a victorious, abiding life is that which appears to be the *impossible* factor in his life. But the bigger the obstacle the greater the manifestation of God's might. God requires faith in the face of the obstacle, but He will always go before. According to the measure that one follows God's leadership, he will personally experience His might. And just as Joshua was

[20]The reported blockage of the Jordan in 1927 by a landslide does not demand that the event of Joshua took place in the same manner.

[21]The location is identified here, proleptically, as Gilgal, though it was not given this name until later (5:9*b*).

God's representative leader, walking with his people and bringing them over, so Jesus, the Captain of our faith, invites the Christian to warm, intimate fellowship and sure, loving guidance by obeying His simple call, "Follow me."

III. SPIRITUAL PREPARATION (5:2-15)

Israel was not yet fully prepared to enter into battle on the soil of Canaan. The unfinished business was spiritual in character. Partly, it involved the observance of Moses' law (cf. 1:7-8); wholly, it was Israel's heart relationship to Jehovah. This chapter records four experiences which God brought to Joshua and the people, each one centered about a token, or symbol: circumcision, blood, fruit, and a sword.

A. The Token of Circumcision: Restoration to covenant favor (5:2-9)

The covenant promise of God to Israel had been temporarily suspended during the nearly forty years' judgment of exclusion from Canaan because of Israel's sin. Since the judgment was a national one, everyone, including young people and babies born in the wilderness, had to live in the environment of a punished nation. Until the ban would be lifted, the rite of circumcision, which was the *token of God's covenant* between Himself and His people (Gen. 17:11),[22] was purposeless, and so the rite was discontinued (5:4-6). Now that the ban was officially lifted, on Israel's entrance into Canaan, the day to renew the rite and restore the nation to positional

[22]Read Genesis 17:9-14 for the record of the first circumcision and its significance.

relationship of covenant favor had arrived. And so Joshua, at the command of God, had all the children of Israel circumcised.[23] The reproach of Egyptians who scoffingly suggested that God had delivered Israel from Egypt in order to slay them in the mountains (Exodus 32:12) was now rolled away (5:9a). As a historical marker for this bright new day, the area was appropriately named Gilgal (literally "rolling off or away").

B. The Token of Blood: Anticipation of deliverance (5:10)

Israel's first Passover was observed in Egypt (Exodus 12:1-20). The slaying of the paschal lamb, and the applying of the blood to the doorposts and lintels, anticipated deliverance from the oppression of that land. The blood was a token assuring such deliverance: "And the blood shall be to you for a token . . . and when I see the blood, I will pass over you" (Exodus 12:13). Israel's second Passover was observed in the wilderness, when hopes of reaching the land were high (Num. 9:5). Now, as the people of a new generation reached Canaan and recalled from history how God delivered their forefathers out of Egypt, they also could anticipate deliverance in the battles to come, as the lamb was slain for the Passover. The circumcision rite was for positional relationship; this Passover sacrifice was for stirring up hopes of deliverance.

C. The Token of Fruit: Appropriation of the blessings (5:11-12)

Manna, the daily food which God supernaturally gave

[23]The terms "again" and "second time" of verse 2 refer to the reinstatement of the rite.

Israel during her desert and wilderness years up to the day of Passover at Gilgal, now ceased (5:12). Manna was a miraculous provision to sustain through a difficult journey, but now Israel could begin to enjoy the changed diet of the fruits of the land of Canaan, the first token of the wealth of blessings promised them in this land of milk and honey. And so, "on the very next day after the Passover, they ate what was raised on the land, unleavened bread and parched grain" (5:11, Berkeley Version). The fruit of the land was a foretaste of blessings to come.

D. The Token of a Sword: Revelation of a holy war (5:13-15)

The circumcision, the Passover, and the produce of the land were intended for the edification of all the Israelites. Now their leader Joshua was given a divine revelation, experienced by him alone, but passed on subsequently to his people.

As Joshua was looking in the direction of the fortress of Jericho, he thought of one thing, his responsibility in the battle. In mind's eye he envisioned the two foes, Canaanites and Israelites, in mortal combat, and though he had already been given assurances of victory, he could not avoid wondering about the outcome as he compared the military strength of both. The closer the hour of actual combat, the more he felt that this was *his* war. At such a critical moment he saw ahead of him a man holding a drawn sword. The drawn sword told Joshua that whatever the man was up to, or had to say, concerned battle. Joshua approached him with the challenge "Art thou for us, or for our adversaries?"

(5:13). The conversation that ensued did not produce a direct answer to that question as such, but put into focus that which Joshua needed to see very clearly at this time, that the *battle was not his but the Lord's.* The man identified himself as the prince of Jehovah's host, suggesting that he came with a message from God (5:14). With this identification Joshua now sensed the crisis of the moment, and, prostrating himself before the prince, besought as a servant the message from his Lord. The message was short but urgent: "Put off thy shoe from off thy foot; for the place whereon thou standest is holy" (5:15). Canaan ground was holy ground. A battle fought over it by God's people for the fulfillment of God's promise was *God's* battle, a holy war. This was not Joshua's war! What a tremendous revelation to God's servant given at the commencement of battle. And Joshua removed his shoe, for the place was holy, and he revered it.

*   *   *

The Christian who sincerely desires to live his life in God's blessed will and favor—in God's rest-land—will find that it is not he living the life, but Christ living in him. Therefore, in the face of all the enemies of his soul who would keep him from this living relationship to Christ as Lord, he must prepare his heart. First, has unconfessed sin broken fellowship with God, causing a suspension of claim to His blessing? Confession will mark the day of reproach rolled away. Then, is there a lurking doubt whether God will give the victories He has promised, because of unworthiness? When God sees the blood of Jesus His Son, He passes over and delivers. Perhaps the Christian has been hesitant to partake of a token of the blessings of Canaan land. He needs but taste and see! The fruit of the land is so much more delightful than the manna of the desert. And if the weight of battle against Satan and his hosts is too heavy to bear, the Son of God goes before to wage His holy war, to meet "the tyrant's brandished steel." One has nothing to lose, and all to gain!

The Israelites on the plain of Jericho had committed themselves when they crossed the divided Jordan and watched it close behind them. Practically speaking, they had reached a point of no return. But they were not led here to be shut up to a life of squalor, shame, and subjugation; rather, a glorious land lay open before them—a land for them to enjoy with its milk and honey, its homes and temples for the worship of God. The yesterdays were days of preparation; the tomorrows would be days of conquest. Written in the skies above were the timeless words of the mandate, "Go in to possess the land, which Jehovah your God giveth you" (Joshua 1:11). And God's people of generations later have been joining in the spirit of commitment to such a life by saying, with the writer of Hebrews, "Let us therefore give diligence to enter into that rest" (Heb. 4:11).

PART TWO

THE CONQUEST
(6:1—12:24)

I. THE CENTRAL CAMPAIGN (6:1—8:35)
   A. Victory Through Faith: Jericho (6:1-27)
   B. Defeat Through Sin: Ai (7:1-26)
   C. Restoration (8:1-35)

II. THE SOUTHERN CAMPAIGN (9:1—10:43)
   A. Alliance with Gibeon (9:1-27)
   B. War Against the Five Kings (10:1-27)
   C. Other Conquests (10:28-43)

III. THE NORTHERN CAMPAIGN (11:1-15)

IV. SUMMARY (11:16—12:24)
   A. Summary of the Canaan Campaigns (11:16-23)
   B. Summary of the Kings Smitten (12:1-24)
   C. Recapitulation

Part Two

THE CONQUEST

(6:1–12:24)

To POSSESS CANAAN meant to drive out the enemy. But the enemy were many—Hittites, Amorites, Perizzites, Jebusites, and others—each to be reckoned with as Joshua planned his strategy of conquest. There is no record of God explicitly instructing Joshua as to the pattern of that strategy, though divine direction was ever-present. Actually, the geographical location of entrance into the north-south-oriented Canaan, at Jericho, determined the plan. See map on page 8 for the general movements of the central, southern, and northern campaigns. The strategy was simply to (1) gain the bridgehead at Jericho; (2) extend the battle in this central region to effect a wedge between the northern and southern armies; (3) then engage each, one after the other, the nearer armies (southern) first. The account of the book of Joshua follows the sequence of that plan in recording the highlights[1] of Israel's conquest of the enemies in Canaan. The following chart outlines this section of Joshua:

[1]As with all history in the Bible, selectivity, not exhaustiveness, is the aim. Those events are recorded which retain the unity of the narrative and serve the underlying purposes of the divine revelation. In the book of Joshua, not all the events but the highlights of the campaigns are recorded.

THE CONQUEST
6:1–12:24

6:1			9:1	11:1	11:16 12:24
CENTRAL CAMPAIGN			SOUTHERN CAMPAIGN	NORTHERN CAMPAIGN	SUMMARY
	7:1	8:1			
Victory Through Faith	Defeat Through Sin	Restoration	Progressive Conquests		

There is a marked crescendo of triumph throughout the seven-year[2] period of battle, after a serious setback at Ai (chap. 7) in the early central campaign.

I. THE CENTRAL CAMPAIGN (6:1–8:35)

A. Victory Through Faith: Jericho (6:1-27)[3]

Although the Jordan miracle impressed the Israelites with awe, the Jericho miracle had all the elements of the colorful and spectacular about it. *Sounds* were part of the action: sounds of the daily march; sounds of the priests' trumpets; the "sound of silence" as no word was spoken (6:10); the chattering of the people after the

[2]John C. Whitcomb, in the chart *Old Testament Patriarchs and Judges*, writes, "The conquest was completed in seven years according to Caleb (Joshua 14:7, 10)."
[3]Suggested outline for this chapter: (1) Assurance and instructions (1-7); (2) The seven days of marching (8-21); (3) Spared of the city (22-25); (4) Curse (26-27).

march each day, wondering what was coming up next (for Joshua apparently did not tell the people of the miracle they were to behold); and, climactically, the shout of the hosts and the thunderous crash of the walls. *Sights* were also part of the spectacular setting: the sight of the imposing mud-brick fortress, behind whose shut gates cowered a fear-stricken nation; the sight of the Israelite army in march, with the priests and ark between the forward and rear contingents; the breathtaking sight of the crumbling walls; and the red flames and black smoke of an entire city punished by God.

Why such a spectacle? What was God teaching? Whom was He teaching?

First of all, the pageantry of God's audio-video lesson could not have been planned to stir Jericho to action. Nor could there have been a military purpose to weaken Jericho by a suspense of six days, for Jericho's morale had already collapsed, as Joshua knew. And, whether the enemy's reaction during the six days of Israel's marching was one of bewilderment or even hope of mercy, they were doomed to die within a week; punishment, not reparation, was their lot. The biblical account itself indicates that Jericho's people were not the object of God's teaching. Throughout the chapter there is no record of any action by them; they merely waited, and then were slain and burned. In fact, the opening words of the chapter are prophetically ominous: "Now Jericho was straitly shut up . . . none went out, and none came in" (6:1).

It is very clear that God's instructions to Joshua for taking Jericho in such a dramatic way were for Israel's benefit. The account in chapter 6 reveals these lessons for Israel:

1. *Unquestioning Obedience*

God's instructions to Joshua as to this strange procedure in taking Jericho (6:2-5) elicited no questions from Joshua. He might have asked, "Why marching and not fighting?" "Why extend this over several days?" "Why silence?" "Why the shout?" But if he wanted God's end in the design, he must accept God's method. Likewise, it was sufficient for Israel to hear Joshua's instructions to march (6:6-11), and then, in enlightened faith, to obey. Had not God magnified Joshua as their leader? Answers to questions could await a future day; faith and obedience alone would light their present path.

2. *Bond of Unity*

The march around the city[4] must have impressed the army of Israel with the might of their unity. They had not marched like this before—the journey through the wilderness was not a military march! True, this was no parade of West Point precision. But the procession had about it the warmth of souls knit together by a common task in the face of a common foe.

3. *Necessity for Undefilement*

Israel needed to learn that there was defilement for partaking of things of the heathen nations confiscated in war contrary to directions from God. An interesting use of the Hebrew word *herem* is made in this account.

[4]One can walk around the nine-acre mound at the site in fifteen to twenty minutes. See *The Wycliffe Bible Commentary*, p. 213.

The city of Jericho and its contents were "devoted" (*herem*) or assigned to Jehovah for His sovereign disposition (6:17). These were not to be appropriated by the Israelites ("keep yourselves from the devoted [*herem*] thing"), lest the camp be "accursed" (*herem*) for the legal defilement (6:18).[5] God's purpose for the silver and gold and the vessels of brass and iron was to place them into the service of the priests ("treasury of Jehovah," 6:19), whereas His disposition of the city itself, including all its inhabitants and livestock, was to "utterly" destroy (*herem*) it (6:21). The temptation of Israel in the wake of victory over a heathen nation was to covet the booty and presume sovereign disposition of it. But God was the Conqueror, with sole rights of confiscation. Israel must keep herself pure from heathen defilement.

4. Renewed Vision of God

God is never stingy in the revelation He gives of Himself to mankind. Since leaving the plain of Moab, Israel had seen much of God and of His works. Now, at Jericho, He was to reveal more, including:

His constant presence. The intimacy of His presence, His dwelling-among, was visibly symbolized by locating the ark in the midst of the warriors, with a contingent ahead of the ark (6:7), and a rear element following the ark (6:9).

His sovereignty. The battles of Israel were God's battles against His enemies, fought through His people for His people. The ram's horns blown by the priests were not military trumpets, but jubilee trumpets, such as were

---

[5]*The Wycliffe Bible Commentary* suggests 6:18b be read, "lest ye covet and take some of the devoted portion."

usually associated with the year of jubilee, for this was a religious, not a military undertaking.

His thoroughgoing demands. The Israelites were learning again and again that there were no halfway measures with God. He promised *all* of Canaan to Israel. He punished *all* unbelievers in the wilderness for their disobedience. He demanded that *all* tribes help in the conquest. Circumcision was to be restored to *all* male Israelites. *All* the law must be kept. *All* the heart must seek after God. Here, at Jericho, *all* the people were to shout, the city was *utterly* destroyed, even to the extent of pronouncing a curse on its future restorer (6:26).[6] The number seven, a number of wholeness and completeness, symbolized this aspect of God's nature. There were to be seven days of marching, seven encirclings on the seventh day, and seven priests blowing seven horns (6:3-4).

His omnipotence. The miracle itself spoke vividly of this. Whether or not God used secondary causes, such as an earthquake, to fell Jericho's walls,[7] the event itself was wholly miraculous. For the timing was foretold by God (6:5): on the seventh day, at the end of the seventh march, at the moment of the people's shout, the walls would fall down in their place. "And it came to pass" (6:20).

[6]Fulfilled in the time of King Ahab (I Kings 16:34). The substance of the curse of Joshua 6:26 was that refortification was forbidden, though resettlement was allowed (e.g., in the occupation of Benjamin's tribe, 18:21).

[7]Just as some hold to the secondary cause of a landslide in the damming of the Jordan River (e.g., interpreting the phrases "the earth trembled" [Judges 5:4] and "the mountains skipped like rams" [Ps. 114:4] as poetic descriptions of such natural phenomena).

His holy wrath. Israel was not by nature a warlike people, and to engage in such an extensive military campaign on the offensive was not the nation's choice, but a mandate from God. Knowing why God was punishing the Canaanites gave the Israelites a keener knowledge of His holy person. The annihilation of the entire population of Canaanite cities was purposed by God to purge the land of the Israelites' future dwellingplace of all the corruption of its heathen polytheism. Religious prostitution, infant sacrifice, and many other corrupt and brutal practices were potentially fatal threats to the righteous life of Israel in Canaan, and it was for Israel's benefit that God commanded the purge. Furthermore, the slaughter of all the inhabitants of Jericho—young and old, with the exception of Rahab and her household (6:21-22)—was totally justifiable on the basis of the sovereign right of the holy Creator to design life from its beginning to its end, which design included the *unmixability of sin and holiness*. The wars of Israel against the idolatrous nations of Canaan were God's holy wars, and their disposition of the prisoners was the fulfillment of God's orders. If only Israel had learned for her future days that *her* idolatry too would reap the vengeance of the same holy God!

* * *

The lessons for Israel at Jericho are beneficial for the Christian today. Faith and obedience to instructions from God will see the fortress of the enemy of the soul crumble under the mighty hand of the Lord. For this purpose the "Son of God [was] manifested, that he might destroy the works of the devil" (I John 3:8).

B. Defeat Through Sin: Ai (7:1-26)[8]

1. *The Sin* (7:1*a*)

The glamorous victory of Jericho, God's blessing on the people, and Joshua's spreading fame (6:27) were all short-circuited by sin during the hours after the enemy was taken, as the spoils were being gathered for the treasury of Jehovah. A secret sin was committed at Jericho; its judgment was withheld by God until Israel made contact with its next enemy at Ai. Joshua had made it very clear to his people that while God had "given" them the city (6:16), everything in it was devoted (*herem*) to God (6:17) for His disposition,[9] and to take of the *herem* was to "make the camp of Israel accursed, and trouble it" (6:18). Disobeying the injunction, Achan, of the tribe of Judah, secretly stole some of the spoil (7:1, 21), thereby defiling the entire camp of Israel: "the children of Israel committed a trespass [literally 'acted faithlessly'] in the devoted thing" (7:1). The crime itself was imputed to all of Israel, because of the integrated relationship of this family of God who had collectively accepted the terms of taking Jericho but who now had broken the covenant in the person of one man, Achan.

2. *The Consequences* (7:1*b*-9)

Wrath of God (7:1*b*). The consequences of the sin were far-reaching. The ultimate judgment fell not only on Achan but on all Israel: "The anger of Jehovah was kindled against the children of Israel" (7:1*b*). The his-

[8]A simple broad outline for Chapter 7: The Event (7:1-5); The Query (7:6-9); The Disposition (7:10-26).
[9]Cf. 6:19, 21. Not only the *things* of Jericho but the *people* also were God's, subject to His sovereign disposition.

tory of Israel could have ended here—even though its most recent battle had been a victory (Jericho)—if this anger had not been turned away. It is to be noted that the wrath of God was kindled at the moment of Achan's sin, but Joshua and all of Israel were not yet aware of either the sin or the judgment.

Defeat of the army (7:2-5a). Exulting in his victory over Jericho, and unaware of the impending divine judgment, Joshua lost no time in preparing for battle against Ai, about ten miles west of Jericho.[10] His spies, unenlightened of God, delivered an inaccurate report of Ai's strength by underestimating their number ("They are but few," 7:3), when actually there were 12,000 men (8:25). Joshua therefore sent only three thousand men to Ai, who were immediately repulsed by the hosts of Ai and chased eastward as far as the defiles in the cliffs. Israelite casualties were thirty-six deaths, plus more perhaps "at the descent."[11]

Demoralizing of the nation (7:5b). The setback of Joshua's army at Ai was a minor loss compared to what happened to the people's morale. The text reads, "And the hearts of the people melted, and became as water" (7:5b). One can understand the cause for such defeat of spirit. The last thing Israel knew before this defeat, God was with Joshua, favoring the people. *To their knowledge,* nothing had transpired to alter the favor. Had God changed?

---

[10]Ai, a city of the hill-country Amorites, was strategically located on the eastern edge of the central ridge, just two miles east of Bethel, and commanding the main route from Gilgal by the Jordan to Bethel and its environs.

[11]Berkeley Version: "killed more on the way down" (7:5); "more" is a paraphrase of the original text, however.

Upset of the leader (7:6-9). In sharp contrast to the defeatism of the people's melted hearts was the upset and bewilderment of their leader as he prostrated himself before God, searching the mind of God and His designs for Israel. "And Joshua rent his clothes, and fell to the earth upon his face before the ark of Jehovah until the evening, he and the elders of Israel; and they put dust upon their heads" (7:6). In his confrontation with God, Joshua, exasperated, alternated between questions and exclamations as he unburdened his heart:

QUESTION: Why have You brought us here, only to perish at the hands of the Amorites? (7:7*a*)

EXCLAMATION: Would that we had been content to dwell beyond the Jordan (7:7*b*)

QUESTION: What shall I say, after Israel has retreated from her enemies? (7:8)

EXCLAMATION: The Canaanites will cut off our name from the earth! (7:9*a*)

QUESTION: What will You do for Your great name? (7:9*b*)

There is a notable omission from Joshua's questions. He does not seek a cause for the defeat at Ai. He apparently attributes it to sovereign design, and asks only the reason for such design. But his last question is the crucial one. It reveals that Joshua has not abandoned his faith in God his Commander-in-chief. His only question is, what will God *now* do to continue to exalt His Name? In fact, the answer to this question is the answer to the other questions.

3. *The Revelation* (7:10-15)

God's explanation (7:10-12*a*). After rebuking Joshua

for unpurposefully prostrating himself on the ground,[12] God answered the question not voiced by Joshua, as to the explanation of the setback: "Israel hath sinned" (7:11). Since Joshua was still not aware what that sin was, God elaborated on the details of the transgression, making it very clear that it was a corporate sin of the nation,[13] in stealing and hoarding "the devoted thing." That was the *sin*. The *judgment* was made just as clear: "Therefore . . . Israel cannot stand," having become accursed under the laws of the sacred portion. Therefore Jehovah said, "I WILL NOT BE WITH YOU ANY MORE" (7:12). Thirteen verses previously the book of Joshua had recorded a glorious picture: "So Jehovah was with Joshua" (6:27). Now, the prospects were nil, but for one hopeful word from God, "EXCEPT," on which the destiny of Israel hinged.

God's proposition (7:12b-15). Righteous judgment on Israel was spelled out. Then God's grace was proposed to the nation, offering restoration of His presence and favor, conditional upon Israel's fulfillment of His "except" (7:12b). The one condition laid upon Israel was getting rid of the devoted thing among them, the very cause of their defilement. The process of the purge was programed by God as the order of the next day, and involved the following:

---

[12]It should be noted that Joshua's prostration before Jehovah was not for any sin of Israel, such as was often the reason for Moses' prostration (cf. Num. 16:4). Jehovah's rebuke, "Get thee up," is followed immediately by the sharp indictment, "Israel hath sinned" (7:10-11).

[13]Notice the repetition, for emphasis, of "they have even" (7:11).

1. *The People's Sanctification* (7:13).

This was preparation of heart and mind to engage in the morrow's divine purge.

2. *The Transgressor's Identification* (7:14, 16-18).

Only God knew Achan to be the transgressor, and He chose to reveal the culprit by the method of drawing lots.[14] Because the screening of the entire nation could be a long and laborious task, an efficient process of elimination was stipulated, progressing from the large unit to the smaller: tribes, families (clans), households, and individuals. The lots drawn on the following day fell to the tribe of Judah, then the family of the Zerahites, of this family the household of Zabdi, and finally the man Achan: "and Achan . . . was taken" (7:18).

Part of the identification of the transgressor involved his own confession of the sin, which publicly confirmed the supernatural exposure of the guilty one. Joshua's warmhearted though firm charge to Achan (7:19) and Achan's honest confession of covetousness (7:20-21) provide touching insight into the sober reflections of two souls (one innocent, one guilty) concerning sin:

JOSHUA'S *tenderness:* "my son"
　appeal: "I pray thee"
　glorification of God: "give glory to Jehovah"
ACHAN'S *honesty:* "of a truth"
　sense of guilt: "I have sinned against Jehovah"

---

[14]The word *taketh* may be interpreted as meaning "indicates by lot" (so reads Berkeley Version). The lot drawn was not of chance, but of *divine* identification: "the tribe which Jehovah indicates by lot" (7:14, Berkeley). (Cf. I Sam. 14:41-42; Num. 26:55; Acts 1:26).

admission of weakness: "I saw . . . coveted . . . took . . . hid"[15]

3. *The Transgressor's Judgment* (7:12-13, 15, 22-25).

God's proposition of Israel's restoration to favor was not on the basis of excusing and overlooking the sin. All sin reaps judgment. It was only on the basis of exact penalty paid (by Achan) that those to whom the sin was imputed (Israel) could be delivered. And so the condition for restored favor with God was the destruction of the stolen spoil and the death of Achan, "he and all that he hath; because he hath transgressed the covenant of Jehovah, and because he hath wrought folly in Israel" (7:15). After Achan's confession, the stolen things were recovered from Achan's tent by Joshua's messengers. Whereupon Joshua and Israel, represented by its leaders, brought the *herem* things, Achan, his children,[16] his cattle and possessions, to a valley site away from the camp of Israel. Here Achan, whose name means "troubler,"[17] heard the final words of judgment: "Why hast thou troubled us? Jehovah shall trouble thee this day." Then the fatal stones rained on him and his children, and all his possessions were burned with fire

---

[15]Joshua first heard specifically from Achan what he had stolen of the spoils: a beautiful mantle of Shinar (Babylon), which may have been woven with gold threads and thus assigned to God's treasury; two hundred shekels of silver (the equivalent of two hundred silver dollars); and a bar of gold of fifty shekels weight (the equivalent of five hundred dollars).

[16]In view of the law cited in Deuteronomy 24:16 prohibiting the execution of children for their father's sins, we assume the children must have had a part in Achan's sin and therefore were guilty of death. Some interpreters do not see their execution included in 7:25.

[17]I Chron. 2:7 reads, "Achar, the troubler of Israel. . . ."

(7:25). Desiring to keep the warning against sinning in the camp ever before them, the Israelites built a historical marker of a great heap of stones over his body, and named the place "Valley of Achor," or "Valley of Troubling."

4. *The Reinstatement* (7:26).

Israel, in fulfilling the conditions for renewed relationship with God, could now claim the fulfillment of His promise of favor. Chapter 7 opens with the dark picture of the Lord's righteous anger kindled against His people; the last verse restores the bright prospects for eventual conquest of God's rest-land: "and Jehovah turned from the fierceness of his anger" (7:26).

C. Restoration (8:1-35)

1. *Restored Courage:* Conquest of Ai (8:1-29)

Achan's sin shattered the momentum which Israel had attained in its miraculous marches across a river and around a city. Israel's courage was gone, its hope all but faded. But God, having now turned from the fierceness of His wrath, set about to accomplish another work of grace and thereby restore the people's courage.

God's encouragement (8:1-2). Tenderly, because He was speaking to a broken heart, God said to Joshua, "Fear not, neither be thou dismayed." The words were spoken, albeit tenderly, with the same power and authority as when Jesus commanded dead Lazarus to come forth from the tomb, and they suggest that God was reaching far down to lift up a soul out of the depths of fear and despair. How else can one explain Joshua's immediate response to the command in positive action: "So Joshua arose" (8:3*a*)?

Restoration is simply returning. When fellowship with God is broken by sin, restoration of that fellowship comes by returning to the place of separation, confessing the sin, and renewing the walk with God from there. In the case of the Israelites, Achan's sin, though committed at Jericho, took its toll at Ai, since Jericho fell before the sin. So the place of renewed walk would be at Ai.[18] Thus God's instructions to Joshua were "Go up to Ai." It was a journey of about fifteen miles from Gilgal, an ascent of 3,200 feet, and the journey would recall all the intimidating pictures of the recent flight from Ai. But Ai was the place for Israel to regain her momentum. In fact, God promised to restore the pre-Ai momentum to Israel by assuring her of victory *as at Jericho.* He told Joshua, "I have given into thy hand the king of Ai"— even as earlier He had said to Joshua, "I have given into

---

[18]Much has been written about the exact location of Ai, since modern archaeological excavations have revealed that et-Tell, the site usually identified with Ai, which was destroyed by the Amorites around 2000 B.C. and was not rebuilt until around 1200 B.C., did not exist when Joshua entered the land (around 1400 B.C.). If et-Tell was the site of a pre-2000 B.C. Ai, the Ai which Joshua conquered may have been located at a nearby site, having had the older Ai name transferred to it, a common procedure in Palestine, according to Sir Frederic Kenyon (Merrill F. Unger, *Unger's Bible Dictionary* [Chicago: Moody Press, 1957], p. 36). Other explanations have been offered. W. F. Albright suggests that Bethel is the Ai of chapter 8 (but the text clearly distinguishes between Bethel and Ai). Others assume that Ai was merely the location of a military outpost of the Bethelites (but the text clearly refers to an inhabited, fortified city with a king). While the exact location of Ai has not been satisfactorily determined, there is no question but that in Joshua's day it was an inhabited, fortified city, ruled over by a king, and located near Bethel. The study of the biblical text is in no way hindered or jeopardized by this unsettled question of Ai's location.

thy hand Jericho" (6:2). Also, He said very explicitly,
"And thou shalt do to Ai . . . *as* thou didst unto Jericho
. . ." (8:2*a*).

Test of courage (8:3-13). The measure of courage is
in the test. God assured Joshua that he would take Ai,
but there would not be the ease of watching its walls
fall as at Jericho. Instead, the manner assigned was by
military ambush, which meant danger, suspense, pre-
caution, and alertness. This was Israel's test of courage,
and Joshua and the warriors rose to the challenge (8:3).

Joshua's strategy involved two ambuscades. The first
group, a contingent of thirty men of valor,[19] was sent
forth one day prior to the battle (8:9). The men were
to hide just west of the city, and be ready for the signal
of advance (8:4). Their assignment was not primarily
to battle hand to hand, but to enter the city and burn it
after its warriors had deserted to chase Joshua and his
army to the east (8:5-8). The second ambush of five
thousand men was positioned also west of Ai, between
it and Bethel,[20] but very likely closer to Bethel than the
first ambush. The purpose of this fighting force becomes

[19]The size of this group is indicated by the text as 30,000 men,
which appears to be an unusually large contingent for such a secret
maneuver as ambush close to the city. One plausible answer to
the problem is that the text should read "thirty officers." This suggestion is made by R.E.D. Clark, who points out that the Hebrew
word *'elep,* translated "thousand," can also be translated as "chief"
or "officer," as it is translated in other passages (cf. I Chron. 12:23-
27; II Chron. 13:3, 17; 17:14-19). If this were the case, then the
thirty-man group was a highly selected commando unit, assigned
to enter the vacated city and burn it. This view may better explain
also the description of the contingent as chosen for being "mighty
men of valor"—more meaningful to a thirty-man group than to a
30,000-man unit. It should be noted here, however, that the second ambuscade definitely involved 5,000 men (8:12).

[20]Bethel was situated about three miles west of Ai, with hill
ranges between.

apparent when one considers that Bethel and Ai had very likely pledged themselves to each other in a defense pact, in the event one of them was attacked. Joshua therefore had to be ready also to meet an army of Bethelites coming from the west. This no doubt was part of the assignment given to this 5,000-man ambush (in addition to their meeting the Ai-ites in the field, 8:22). As it turned out, Joshua's strategy was wisely planned, for "there was not a man left in Ai *or* Bethel, that went not out after Israel" (8:17).[21]

The third contingent of Joshua's overall plan was the decoy of warriors, which he personally would lead. This group encamped on the north side of Ai, in plain view of the city, with a valley between them and the city. That night Joshua moved into the valley with his army, to indicate to the men of Ai their intentions of war (8:13). Ai's king took the bait, and prepared for battle at dawn (8:14).

The key to victory at Ai was the courage of the Israelites lying in wait for the battle. These were hours of waiting that must have drawn out like agonizing days, both for the two ambuscades, and the leading decoy. God's tests of men's faith often are prolonged, but always with purpose!

Courage in battle (8:14-24). Suspense usually gives way to release at the moment of combat, but this was not Israel's experience at Ai for the simple reason of the strategy of ruse. For they had to act as if they were beaten before Ai, fleeing by way of the desert wilderness

---

[21]Actually, therefore, the battle of Ai was also a battle against Bethel, and the neutralizing of Bethel's army at this time made it unnecessary for Joshua to capture the city itself immediately (cf. Judges 1:22-26).

with all of Ai on their heels (8:15-16). This was the
climax of the test of their courage and faith, for there
must have arisen the fear that perhaps their flight was
real. But the long minutes of retreat finally came to an
end when, at God's direction, Joshua gave the prear-
ranged signal to the ambush group by raising his javelin,[22] the signal for them to take the city and burn it
(8:18-19). When the Ai-ites saw behind them the smoke
of their city pouring into the skies, consternation and
utter frustration gripped them. With no way to turn,
and with the Israelites closing in from both sides, it was
just a matter of time before all were slain by the edge
of the sword. Only the king was spared for the moment,
reserved for the ignoble death of hanging (8:20-24, 29).

The rewards (8:25-29). For faith and courage to trust
God in a second attempt against Ai after the disgrace of
defeat, Joshua and his people won the rewards of conquest. The enemy was obliterated (12,000 men and
women); Ai (literally "heap") was made "a heap for
ever, even a desolation" (8:28); and over the king's dead
body was raised a heap of stones to be a standing memorial of another milestone of Israel's history: defeat followed by victory. The material reward given the Israelites was the cattle and spoils of the battle, as promised by God, to help sustain the nation in its continued
advances (8:27).

2. *Renewed Consecration:* Altar at Ebal (8:30-35)[23]

[22]The *kidon* (translated "javelin") which Joshua raised might
have been a scimitar, whose shiny blade would serve as the sun's
reflector for a long distance.
[23]Some feel that the events at Ebal took place at the close of the
conquest, after all the land was subdued, and are related here by
anticipation. However, there is sound reason for regarding the

When Israel was still encamped at Moab, waiting to cross over into Canaan, Moses gave as one of his last instructions the order to set up an altar at Ebal when Israel crossed over the Jordan: "When ye are passed over the Jordan . . . ye shall set up these stones, which I command you this day, in mount Ebal (Deut. 27:4; Joshua 8:31). Joshua's fidelity to God, to Israel, and to Moses was demonstrated in his losing no time in obeying the instructions by leading the people to Ebal after Ai's fall. While Moses did not specify how soon after the Jordan crossing the altar would have to be set up, the spirit of the charge was that there should be no delay. From a purely military standpoint Joshua might have reasoned, after taking Ai, that there needed to be a more extensive destruction of the enemy peoples in the central sector before he could hope to march his people the two days' journey northward to Ebal. But Joshua, faithful and obedient servant that he was, knew that the next order of business was not battles but altars. The journey of Israel—men, women, children, cattle, and possessions—from Gilgal northward to Ebal must have been uneventful, for the account of Joshua makes no reference to it. The route taken was probably along the Jordan plains where there were no major fortresses, and then westward from Adam to the amphitheater location of Shechem, on both sides of which stood the "spectator" mounts, Ebal to the north (elevation 3,085') and Gerizim to the south (elevation 2,890'). That Israel did not have to battle with the people in the fortress at Shechem may be explained by the fact that the city was

events as happening at this early time, in view of Moses' instructions.

in friendly hands (cf. 20:7; 24:1),[24] or that the size of
the group there was insignificant.[25]

Original instructions (Joshua 8:31; Deut. 27:1-26).
God, using His favorite method of object lesson in teaching Israel, chose to dramatize the importance of the law
and sacrifice in the new land by prescribing an impressive ceremony in the setting of the two prominent twin
mounts, Ebal and Gerizim. Two mounts were chosen
because the dual lesson of curse and blessing was to be
taught. The geographical location of the mounts was
also undoubtedly with purpose, for, located dead center
in Canaan, they represented the *whole* of the land. The
significance of what Israel was to do therefore involved
her entire existence—whether in battle, or in the subsequent days of dwelling in peace. The instruction called
for the building of two stone structures: one, a stele made
of very large whitewashed stones,[26] on which the words
of the law were written (Deut. 27:2-4, 8); the other, a
stone altar for burnt offerings and peace offerings (Deut.
27:6-7).

Stones for an altar (8:30-31). There is a sharp contrast in the historical sequence of Joshua's account. The
record cites the infamous heap of stones raised at Ai
over the dead body of an idolatrous king (8:29); then,
the very next words report a glorious structure of stones:
"Then Joshua built an altar unto Jehovah, the God of

[24]See *The Wycliffe Bible Commentary*, p. 215.
[25]Shechem apparently did not have a king—at least the list of
thirty-one kings defeated by Joshua does not include such.
[26]Archaeologists have discovered similar stelae made of stones
as long as seven feet. The whitewash or plaster (Deut. 27:2) was
evidently for making a printable surface for the law's recording
(Deut. 27:3).

Israel" (8:30). The stones were unhewn to keep them pure from the pollution of man (Exodus 20:25). On the altar were offered burnt offerings and peace offerings.[27] The burnt offering of the slain animal involved confession of sin, recognition of the death penalty for sin, plea for mercy, and faith that God would accept the sacrifice as an atonement for the offerer's sin (Lev. 1:4). The Israelites at Ebal renewed their dedication to God on this basis. The peace offering was a ceremony of thanksgiving (Lev. 7:11-12), and created an appropriate spirit of rejoicing over God's goodness to the Israelites in their successes thus far. In Moses' instructions was the very clear command "And thou shalt rejoice before Jehovah thy God" (Deut. 27:7).

So at Ebal atonement and thanksgiving spoke from the altar that Joshua built.

Stones for the Law (8:32-35). When the huge stones had been assembled at a spot near the stone altar, Joshua, following Moses' instructions, wrote in the presence of all the Israelites "a copy of the law of Moses" (8:32) ("all the words of this law very plainly," Deut. 27:8).[28] This was Israel's public declaration of dependence on God and determination to let the law of the land be the law of God as spoken through Moses. This commitment to obey the law was dramatized very forcefully in the scene that followed, again according to Moses' earlier

[27]Cf. Lev. 1, 3, 7.

[28]How much of the law was included is difficult to determine. It was not uncommon in ancient times to make lengthy inscriptions on stones and rocks. For example, one has been found at Behistun in Iran, about three times the length of the book of Deuteronomy. At Ebal, more was inscribed than just small parts of Deuteronomy—perhaps as much as all of the legal section of the Pentateuch.

instructions (Deut. 27:11-26). Half the people stood at mount Gerizim[29] to the south, and the other half stood at mount Ebal to the north, with the ark of the covenant and the Levitical priests in between. When all the people were thus positioned, Joshua "read all the words of the law, the blessing and the curse, according to all that is written in the book of the law" (8:34). The six tribes standing at Gerizim symbolized blessing upon the people (Deut. 27:12); the six tribes standing at Ebal symbolized the curse (Deut. 27:13). The point of the dramatization was to reiterate the truth of the two sides of the total law: blessing for obedience, curse for disobedience. The Israelites were coming into a land of blessing, but they must not forget that for any disobedience on their part, there would inevitably fall the recompense of the curse. As Joshua, represented by the Levites, read a sentence from the law, whether it involved blessing *or* curse, the people were to respond, "Amen" (Deut. 27:14-26).[30]

Thus another milestone was reached in the programed conquest of Canaan. The people's recognition of the preeminence of the Lord and His Word was surety for success in the engagements to come.

[29]Deuteronomy 27:12 reads "*upon* mount Gerizim," while Joshua 8:33 reads "in front of mount Gerizim." In view of the large number of Israelites, both locations were probably occupied. It is to be observed here also that foreigners (not native-born Hebrews) were included in the family of God (8:33), confirming the fact that the object of God's Word even in that day was not exclusive.

[30]The twelve examples given in Deuteronomy 27 are of the curse type, but a reading into chapter 28 reveals sections on blessing also, which were undoubtedly part of the responsive reading. For further comment on this, see *The New Bible Commentary*, ed. by F. Davidson, A. M. Stibbs, and E. F. Kevan (Grand Rapids: Wm. B. Eerdmans Pub. Co., 1953), p. 217.

II. THE SOUTHERN CAMPAIGN (9:1–10:43)

The central campaign, now completed, was the key to Israel's conquest of Canaan. Its strategy, as noted earlier, was to drive a wedge through the backbone of Canaan and split in two its theoretically solid frontal line,[31] thereby letting Israel advantageously attack the numerous enemies in two separate campaigns, southern and northern. The critical character of the central campaign explains why proportionately more details of action are recorded in Joshua for this campaign than for the two that followed it. For Israel's first months of battle were months of tests, decisions, identifications of standards, and commitments. There were to be new experiences, but for the most part the momentum and fame of victory had been established. From chapter 10 on there is a noticeable crescendo in the decisive tone of conquest as the frequency of conquests also rises.

The first paragraph of chapter 9 (9:1-2) is really an introduction to both the southern and the northern campaigns, for it reports the effect of Joshua's victories on all the kings of Canaan, from the Jordan to the Great Sea, and from southern Canaan to the northern limits of Lebanon. Earlier, the kings of these nations had despaired when they heard of the miracle of the Jordan (5:1). Perhaps Israel's first setback at Ai prodded them now to hope for successful resistance. And so, counting on the power of alliance, "They gathered themselves together, to fight with Joshua and with Israel, *with one accord*" (9:2).

[31]As indicated earlier, the enemy in Canaan was really many enemies, hence this theoretically solid line was not an integrated front of resistance.

A. Alliance with Gibeon (9:1-27)

1. *Deceit Undetected* (9:3-15)

Gibeon, one of Canaan's "royal cities" and a town of the Hivites, was known by its neighbors as a great city of mighty men, a greater city than Ai (10:2). It was located in the hill country about six miles northwest of Jerusalem and about six miles southwest of Ai. Three neighboring smaller dependent towns, named Chephirah, Beeroth, and Kiriath-jearim, formed a league with Gibeon (9:16-17). Knowing that Israel's God had commanded His people to destroy all the inhabitants of Canaan (9:24), the stratagem of Gibeon was not to resist Israel (the plan of the other Canaanite kings), but somehow to lure Israel into a pact of protection, which would be double insurance, namely, against Israel's army and the armies of the Canaanites.

Craftily moving on the premise of the binding character of a covenant between two parties, a group of Gibeonites, posing as ambassadors from a far country, reached the camp at Gilgal[32] and besought Joshua to enter into a peace covenant with them and their people (9:6-13). They apparently knew that the Israelites were permitted to make peace with nations outside of Canaan (Deut. 20:10-15), though obligated to utterly destroy all Canaanites, so as not to be defiled by their abominations (Deut. 20:16-19).

[32]Some feel that this Gilgal was not the original camping ground of Israel but another Gilgal of Canaan, located southwest of Shiloh. Such a view is based on the assumption that the Israelites would seek a location closer to the future military maneuvers after leaving Ebal. (See Keil and Delitzsch, *op. cit.*, pp. 92-94.) The reading of 10:7-8 seems to indicate, however, that the Israelites returned to the original Gilgal. Its location was certainly more favorable than the Gilgal near Shiloh, from the standpoint of the space demanded for camping so many Israelites.

Joshua and his princes sinned in not seeking "counsel at the mouth of Jehovah" (9:14), through the high priest's inquiry ministry of Urim and Thummim (cf. Num. 27:15-23). The Gibeonites' lie went unrecognized, and Joshua made the covenant of peace with them (9:15).

How carefully the Christian must guard against the cunning deceit of the world in its attempt to get under the protective covert of the Church and capitalize on its blessings. With the Lord's counsel no false overtures need go undetected.

2. *Wrong Discovered* (9:16-17)

Within three days the hoax was exposed, and Israel learned that the Gibeonites dwelt not far from Gilgal. The predicament now facing Israel was twofold: first, Joshua had made an illegal covenant with Canaanites, though in ignorance; second, the covenant being unbreakable by nature, the Gibeonites would have to be spared, but their presence in the midst of Israel, because of their idolatry, could defile the people. How Joshua satisfactorily dealt with both predicaments is the subject of the next two paragraphs of the chapter.

3. *God's Name Protected* (9:18-21a)

The issue over the covenant was not the name or reputation of Israel, but that of Jehovah: "The princes . . . had sworn unto them *by Jehovah, the God of Israel*" (9:18). If the covenant were broken, wrath would come upon Israel (9:20). To preserve the testimony of Jehovah, therefore, the Gibeonites were spared destruction by the Israelite armies (9:21).

4. *Israel's Religion Guarded* (9:21b-27)

Now that it was accepted that the Gibeonites would
be allowed to dwell among the Israelites, the next problem was how to keep the Gibeonites' idolatry from defiling Israel's religion. Joshua's solution was two-pronged.
First, the Gibeonites would be kept from the liberties of
social intercourse among the Israelites, being made wood-
cutters and water carriers at the level of bondservants.[33]
Second, their work was to be done in connection with
the altar of Jehovah and the ministry of the congregation,
where they were not in a position to influence others, but
at the same time could be healthfully exposed to the
revelation of God. That the Gibeonites were blessed in
such an arrangement is confirmed by their usefulness to
God's service in the years that followed,[34] and by the
subsequent exaltation of the *place* Gibeon.[35]

B. War Against the Five Kings (10:1-27)

1. *Amorite Coalition* (10:1-5)

When the king of Jerusalem heard of Joshua's destruction of Ai, and that the mighty Gibeonites had entered
into alliance with Israel, he immediately rallied the support of four other Amorite kings, who brought up their
armies to Gibeon, to make war against it. The kings'
assault on Gibeon was of dual purpose: first, to punish
the Gibeonites for joining the Israelites, and second, to
destroy Israel's newly acquired allied support. The
coalition of five kings was impressive in that it repre-

[33]This was the punishment aspect of Joshua's "curse" (9:23).
[34]Including their helping to rebuild the walls of Jerusalem after
the exile (Neh. 7:25).
[35]See Joshua 10:7-15; I Kings 3:5-15; I Chronicles 21:29;
II Chronicles 1:3.

sented, geographically, the area of southern Canaan which the Israelites needed yet to take.[36] The outcome of the battle with these kings and their armies would be a critical factor in the future of Israel.

2. *The Battle Begun* (10:6-11)

Responding immediately to Gibeon's call for help, Joshua and his army went up from Gilgal under cover of darkness to meet the foe at Gibeon. As on previous occasions, God assured Joshua of complete victory: "Fear them not: for I have delivered them into thy hands; there shall not a man of them stand before thee" (10:8). It was still dark when Joshua reached the vicinity of Gibeon, and he came upon the enemy suddenly. Panic broke out among the armies; many were slain "with a great slaughter"; others fled to the west; and with the Israelites in hot pursuit, God sent a mighty storm of large hailstones upon the Amorites so that more were killed thus than by Israel's sword (10:11). Miraculously also the Israelites were not harmed by the storm.

3. *The Miracle of the Sun and Moon* (10:12-15)

Typical of Hebrew literature, the account of Joshua now reverts back in time, to the early morning hours of "the day when Jehovah delivered up the Amorites before the children of Israel" (10:12). It was at such an hour that Joshua besought of God: "O sun, wait in Gibeon! Wait in the valley of Ajalon, O moon (10:12, Berkeley

---

[36]Locate the five towns on a map to see the area represented. That these five kings *generally* represented *all* of this area of hill-country is indicated by what the Gibeonites said to Joshua: "All the kings of the Amorites that dwell in the hill-country are gathered together against us" (10:6).

Version). His request—*whatever* was involved—was for
military advantage, as indicated by the answer to the
prayer: "The sun waited and the moon stood still, while
a nation took vengeance on its enemies" (10:13*a*).[37]
What the sun (and moon) actually did corresponded to
what Joshua needed from a military standpoint. But
what Joshua needed is not clear from the text; hence the
various explanations offered on this "problem" passage.
Some of the more plausible explanations suggested are:

1) Since Joshua came upon the Amorites by surprise,
apparently in the early hours of dawn, his prayer concerning the sun may have been a request for an *exten-
sion* of the semidarkness and if so, the hailstones sent by
God could have been the answer to that prayer.[38]

2) Joshua needed more daylight time to finish the
battle to its utter completion, and hence was asking for
a prolonged day. This interpretation suggests then that
God held back the earth's rotation while the sun was
above Joshua, making one full rotation to last 48 hours.
Gleason L. Archer says, "It must be admitted that verse
13[*b*] seems to favor a prolongation of the day: 'And
the sun stood in the midst [or midway point] of the sky
and did not hasten to set for a whole day'" (Berkeley
Version).

3) Joshua's exhausted army needed relief from the
merciless heat of the sun, and thus he prayed that the
sun might be made "impotent" in its beating down upon
the troops. This explanation centers about the Hebrew

---

[37]Berkeley Version. Joshua was standing west of Gibeon and
east of Ajalon (10:10) when he spoke these words.

[38]*The New Bible Commentary*, p. 231. According to this interpretation, the Hebrew allows for the translation of 10:13*b* thus:
"The sun made no haste to *come*, about a whole day."

word *dōm*, which is translated "stand thou still" in the
King James Version but means literally "cease" or "leave
off" (as in Lam. 2:18 and II Kings 4:6). The Godsent
hailstorm is thus seen as the answer to Joshua's prayer,
in making the sun "dumb" or impotent.[39]

The first and third explanations cited above demand
that the duration of the hailstorm was unusually long.
This however could account for the exclusive qualifica-
tion cited by 10:14a, "And there was no day like that
before it or after it." The second explanation represents
the common view that the miracle affected the entire
planetary system, an explanation not without problems.

What actually happened is still an open question; that
the phenomenon was unique and miraculous cannot be
denied. Whatever it was that Joshua needed, God gave
it, "for Jehovah fought for Israel" (10:14b).

4. The Battle Completed (10:16-27)[40]

Now the account of the battle against the Amorites is
resumed in the book of Joshua. Fleeing westward from
the hot pursuit of Israel, the five kings hid themselves
in a cave at Makkedah, where they were soon discovered
and held for later disposition (10:16-17). While some

---

[39]See *The Wycliffe Bible Commentary*, p. 218, for a discussion
of this view.

[40]Verse 15 states that Joshua and all Israel returned to Gilgal.
It seems unlikely that such a long journey would be taken by *all*
the Israelites at this point in the campaign. The return to Gilgal
recorded by verse 15 must be the return recorded by verse 43,
since the five kings and other Amorites were still at large. It is
possible that all of 10:12-15 was a quote from the book of Jashar
(except the sentence "Is not this written in the book of Jashar?"),
in which case verse 15 refers to the same return as that of 10:43,
at the end of the southern campaign. The book of Jashar was a
book of poetry honoring heroes of the past.

soldiers remained at Makkedah guarding the prisoners at the cave, the army pursued the Amorites which were still at large, and slew all but those who were able to find refuge in the fortified cities (10:20). At the end of that slaughter Israel's warriors met with Joshua at Makkedah, exulting in their first victory against a coalition of armies. To impress his army with the significance of this victory for their future wars, Joshua, following an eastern custom of conquerors, instructed his chiefs to put their feet on the kings' necks, as a symbol of future victories: "For thus shall Jehovah do to all your enemies against whom ye fight" (10:25). The kings were then smitten, hanged until evening, and cast into the cave, against which were laid great stones—another memorial of the triumphal march of Israel into Canaan.

The Christian intent on living close to God knows all too well that the enemy of his soul is often not one but a coalition of many foes. Who has not faced a coalition of Delusion, Doubt, Discouragement, and Despair; or of Pride, Pomp, and Prejudice; or of Laxity and Lukewarmness? But God is able—"for thus shall Jehovah do to all your enemies against whom ye fight."

C. Other Conquests (10:28-43)

The victory over the five kings and their armies, representing the best of south Canaan, sealed the doom of this part of the land. Joshua and his army went from one city to the next, utterly destroying the city itself and slaying its king and inhabitants, "as Jehovah, the God of Israel, commanded" (10:40). The campaign, which was of considerable duration (cf. 11:18), extended over one period of time without interruption (10:42). Not all the towns of the land were taken during the campaign. Apparently it was not a military necessity that every town be destroyed. The fact that Joshua did not take Jerusalem at this time, however, was later to prove a severe hardship to the tribes of Judah and Benjamin. The list of cities which fell to Joshua is recorded in 10:28-39 in the order in which the battles were fought, generally counterclockwise.[41] The record is brief and matter-of-fact, written in a spirit of decisiveness, and pointing to the key of the success of this large southern campaign:

> And all these kings and their land did Joshua take at one time, because JEHOVAH, THE GOD OF ISRAEL, FOUGHT FOR ISRAEL (10:42)

Now Joshua could look to the unfinished task of the northland with confidence, and in that spirit he returned with his armies to Gilgal to prepare for that mission (10:43).

III. THE NORTHERN CAMPAIGN (11:1-15)

The southern campaign was over, but there was to be no extended period of recuperation for the armies of Israel. Jabin, king of Hazor, a key fortress town north of the Sea of Galilee (Chinnereth), heard of Joshua's crushing victories in the South, and quickly rallied the kings of neighboring towns to the common cause of war with Israel. Included in the coalition forces were remnants of armies routed from the South in Joshua's previous battles: Canaanites, Amorites, Hittites, and others

---

[41]The study of this and other war records in the book of Joshua is enhanced by locating on a map the towns and places cited.

(11:2-3). The number of the combined armies was "as
the sand that is upon the seashore," and in addition they
owned a large number of chariots and horses. "And all
these kings met together; and they came and encamped
together at the waters of Merom" (11:5), just to the
northwest of the Sea of Galilee.

Joshua did not wait for the battle to come to him. He
had already led his armies northward along the Jordan
Valley to within a day's journey from Merom, no doubt
in the region of the Sea of Galilee. He must have
trembled at the prospect of battling such a formidable
foe, with its vast number of warriors besides horses and
chariots.[42] It was then he received the encouraging assurance of victory from God, as he had for previous battles: "Be not afraid of them; for to-morrow at this time
will I deliver them up slain before Israel" (11:6). The
next day in a surprise attack at the waters of Merom the
Israelites fell upon the enemy, chasing them westward
to the coast (towns of Sidon and Misrephoth-maim), and
eastward (valley of Mizpeh), killing all and, at God's
instruction, burning the chariots and laming the horses
(11:9).[43]

Returning from the westward pursuit, Joshua took the
mighty fortress of Hazor, smote its king and people, and
burned the city with fire. He did the same for the other
surrounding cities, except that he did not burn cities
standing on mounds, apparently with the view to their

[42]Josephus says that the northern armies had 300,000 infantry,
10,000 cavalry, and 20,000 chariots (Antiquities V:1:12), though
this may be an exaggeration.
[43]God wanted to keep Israel from building up a military organization to the point where the people would trust in chariots and
horses and not in God (cf. Isa. 31:1).

value to the Israelite tribes which later would be settling in the area.

Joshua's victory in the North was just as decisive as that in the South, and left no question as to who was the giant of the land. Again, obedience to God was the clue to the victory. This is clearly emphasized in the last verse of this section of Joshua: "As Jehovah commanded Moses his servant, so did Moses command Joshua: and so did Joshua; he left nothing undone of all that Jehovah commanded Moses" (11:15).

IV. SUMMARY (11:16–12:24)

As of the close of the northern campaign, it could not be said that *all* the individual towns and kings of Canaan had been conquered by Israel. This is confirmed by God's words to Joshua in 13:1: "There remaineth yet very much land to be possessed." The program of a progressive conquest of Canaan was divinely determined for Israel before she ever got to the land, designed to keep the land from desolation by nature because of a paucity of inhabitants (Exodus 23:28-30; Deut. 7:22). Further, once each of the twelve tribes could settle down in the area allotted to it, it was challenged to drive out the remaining enemies in its own territory. However, in essence Israel had taken Canaan as a whole, and thus it could be written, "So Joshua took all that land" (11:16), and "the land had rest from war" (11:23*b*). The record of Joshua now proceeds to summarize the extent of this "total" conquest in the following order:

A. Summary of the Canaan Campaigns (11:16-23)

1. *Geography* (11:16-17)

The battles were fought over lands that stretched from the Great Sea region ("lowland") on the west to the Arabah (desert south of the Dead Sea) on the east; and from Mount Halak (southwest of the Dead Sea) in the south to Baal-gad (under Hermon) in the extreme north.

2. *Duration* (11:18)

The campaigns lasted for "a long time"—actually about seven years.

3. *Extent* (11:19-20)

All cities encountered were taken in battle; treaty made with none except with Gibeon; Canaanites sought battle, not peace.

4. *Special Mission* (11:21-22)

Special mention is made here of Joshua's defeat of the Anakim, the giants who by their presence in Canaan caused Moses' spies to give a pessimistic report (Num. 13:22, 28, 31, 33).

5. *Summary Statement* (11:23)

"So Joshua took the whole land, according to all that Jehovah spake unto Moses; and Joshua gave it for an inheritance unto Israel according to their division by their tribes. AND THE LAND HAD REST FROM WAR."

B. Summary of the Kings Smitten (12:1-24)

1. *Kings of Transjordan* (12:1-6)

Two kings: Sihon king of the Amorites (12:2) and Og king of Bashan (12:4). These were the kings smitten by Moses, before Israel crossed the Jordan, whose lands were allotted to the tribes of Reuben and Gad and the half-tribe of Manasseh.[44] The geographical extent of this Transjordan acquisition reached from the Arnon River in the south, which was the southern boundary of Sihon's kingdom, to the slopes of Hermon in the north, the land of Bashan, which was Og's kingdom.

2. Kings West of the Jordan (12:7-24)

Thirty-one kings.[45] Their cities were scattered throughout Canaan (the geography is described in verses 7-8), which explains why Israel was engaged in battle for such a long time. The kings are listed in the order in which they were engaged in battle with Joshua.

C. Recapitulation

The seven preceding chapters of Joshua are accounts of wars and conquests. By the time the reader reaches chapter 12, he feels a weariness of the din of arms, and is refreshed by the last short statement of chapter 11: "And the land had rest from war" (11:23). One writer has shared his feelings thus: "The annals of peace are always more brief than the records of war; and when we reach this short but welcome clause we might wish that it were so expanded as to fill our eyes and our hearts with the blessings which peace scatters with her kindly hand."[46]

A good way to relieve the heaviness of soul induced by the record of bloody and devastating battles is to see

[44]Cf. Numbers 21:21 ff.; 32:33 ff.
[45]Gilgal of 12:23 was a different Gilgal from the camping ground of Israel.
[46]William G. Blaikie, *The Book of Joshua* (New York: A. C. Armstrong and Son, 1893), p. 247.

afresh the place of the battles in Israel's history from the
divine overall perspective. A review of the main aspects
of Israel's wars in Canaan forcuses attention on three
things, namely, their origin, agent, and result.

1. The *origin* of the wars was *God*. They were *His*
wars. The man whom Joshua saw with sword in hand
at the commencement of the battles was from God
(5:13). It was *God* who brought Israel to battle, to
purge the land of idolatry. It was *God* who gave Israel
the victory, that she might have a land to dwell in.

2. The *agent* of the wars was *Israel*. A man, Joshua,
and a multitude, the Israelites, were the soldiers and
conquerors and executioners, acting in obedience to their
Commander-in-chief, God. Whatever they did in obedience to His directives had the unique quality of being
holy. This was vividly demonstrated to Joshua, again
at the beginning of the wars, when he was told that the
ground on which he stood was holy (5:15). The land as
well as all that was needed for its conquest was holy.
If the battles were bloody and desolating, they were
holy. If they were many and long, they were holy. God
was using the Israelites to purge and punish idolatrous
nations, and destruction by war was His chosen method.

3. The *result* of the wars was *rest*. The wars were not
the ultimate purpose of God. They were to bring in the
rest. For there could not have been rest for Israel with
idolatrous peoples dwelling in their midst. The phrase
in 11:23 "the land had rest from war" speaks only of rest
negatively. Positively, this was the rest of a dwelling
place in a homeland, of prosperity both materially and
spiritually. It is noteworthy to observe that when God
commissioned Joshua to bring Israel into the land

(1:2-9), the emphasis was on the positive blessings of rest, with only a brief allusion to the conflict aspect of its attainment (1:5).

The major spiritual applications for Christian living are derived from the truths described above. God wants the Christian to enter into rest, to prosper spiritually in the rich environment of His daily blessings. The weights and sins which so easily detain and beset the Christian (Heb. 12:1) need to be dealt with and driven out, for there is no rest in their presence. The Christian intent on living in God's blessings will find that such a life comes not without conflict for the simple reason of the presence of the enemies of the soul. But the battle is really *God's* battle, and the Christian, weak in himself, will find that for faith and obedience to God, God will fight for him, drive out the enemy, give him the victory, and thus let him enjoy the blessings of the rest-land. Rest-living for the Christian is *partaking of Christ* (Heb. 3:14) and looking to Him (Heb. 12:2). All the rest-land blessings stream from His wounded side. In a real sense Jesus has taken the land of promise for His children by His defeat of Satan on the cross, and the Christian's appropriation of Canaan blessings depends on living *in* Him, above the storms and safe from the foes.

PART THREE

THE INHERITANCES
(13:1–21:45)

I. COMMAND TO DIVIDE THE LAND (13:1-7)
  A. Immediate Allotment Because of Joshua's Old Age (13:1a)
  B. Immediate Allotment Despite Partial Conquest (13:1b-7)

II. SPECIAL CONCESSION (to two and one-half tribes) (13:8-33)

III. SPECIAL REWARD I (to Caleb) (14:1-15)
  A. Introduction (14:1-5)
  B. Reward Claimed (14:6-12)
  C. Reward Given (14:13-15)

IV. MAIN INHERITANCE (15:1–19:49a)
  A. Judah (15:1-63)
  B. Sons of Joseph (16:1–17:18)
  C. Seven Remaining Tribes (18:1–19:51)

V. SPECIAL REWARD II (to Joshua) (19:49-51)

VI. SPECIAL CITIES (20:1–21:42)

VII. CONCLUSION (21:43-45)

Part Three

THE INHERITANCES

(13:1–21:45)

THE ACCOUNT OF JOSHUA has now reached a plateau as
far as its content and style are concerned. As noted in
the Introduction of this commentary (see page 15), chapters 1-12 are chapters of *action,* involving preparation for
war (1-5), and then the war itself (6-12). But the ac-
tivities of Israel during those years were not terminal in
themselves. The terminus was reached when it could
be said that "Joshua took the whole land" (11:23) and
that he could now divide the land "for an inheritance
unto Israel according to their divisions by their tribes"
(11:23). The action of the unhappy though necessary
wars was the prelude to the gratifying and pleasant
business of the allotment of the lands to the Israelites.

This section of Joshua concerning the business of allotment may appear on the surface to be bare and unin-
teresting. The multitude of geographical terms contrib-
utes to the difficulty of its study. Two basic approaches
to this problem will help the Bible student immeasurably.
First, he must recognize that whatever is included in the
biblical text—easy or difficult, colorful or mild, exhorta-

tion or history—is divinely intended for the reader's
edification. In its context, small or large, it has something to say about man or God. For example, one should
see in the long listing of geographical names of allotment
the blessed truth that God's promise of Canaan-rest to
His people was a promise to the individual families as
well as to Israel as a whole. Each family was to have
its own home address, as it were. As William Blaikie
has said, "On every one of the places . . . faith may see
inscribed, as in letters from heaven, the sweet word
REST."[1] The second approach which will make the study
of this passage fruitful is the searching for the large
underlying truths undergirding the numerous details,
identifying the timeless universal principles involved.
In the following pages of this commentary, attention is
directed not so much to the details as to those large
substratum truths. The reader is urged to look for other
similar truths.

While there is no record of any pageantry or colorful
ceremony attending the drawing of lots for the land
assignments for each tribe, the importance of such allotments cannot be overstated. This was the climactic
moment in Israel's young life, when for the first time she
could claim a land as her own, given by God. In the
days of the patriarchs—Abraham, Isaac, Jacob, and Joseph—the land was too large for total claim. When by
propagation Israel grew to the size of a formidable nation, the people were dwelling in bondage in a foreign
land, Egypt. The wilderness years were spent on the
way to the land. The seven years of fighting after cross-

[1]William G. Blaikie, *The Book of Joshua* (New York: A. C.
Armstrong and Son, 1893), p. 21.

ing the Jordan were used to conquer the land. Now the hour had come to claim the land, build homes, and live with God in peace. The day of land allotment must have been a happy day indeed!

I. COMMAND TO DIVIDE THE LAND
   (13:1-7)

The command to Joshua to divide the land west of the Jordan is stated at verse 7: "Now therefore divide this land for an inheritance unto the nine tribes, and the half-tribe of Manasseh." Before giving Joshua this order, God gave two explanations regarding his desire to have the allocations made at this time.

A. Immediate Allotment Because of Joshua's Old Age
   (13:1a)

Implied in God's commission to Joshua before he led the Israelites into Canaan was that it was Joshua himself who would divide the inheritance among the tribes (cf. 1:6). Now that Joshua had reached an old age and did not have many more years to live,[2] this was the time for completing that task. He would continue to serve his Master, but from henceforth he would be relieved of the exhausting military labors of leading the nation, for on receiving their individual land assignments the tribes themselves took on the responsibilities of their own land.

B. Immediate Allotment Despite Partial Conquest
   (13:1b-7)

Joshua was to divide the land now, even though there

[2]Joshua died at the age of 110 (24:29). The phrase "old and well stricken in years" in 13:1 and 23:1 must refer to an age relatively close to that.

remained yet "very much land to be possessed" (13:1b).
What that land was is described in verses 2 to 6. It involved mainly the southwest coastal area known in Bible
geography as Philistia (13:2-4a), and the territories to
the far north along the coast (e.g., Sidon) and the peoples of the Lebanon Valley (13:4b-6).[3] The significant
word given to Joshua by God concerning these lands was
that He would drive out their occupants, and that Joshua's present task was to allot the lands, even though
occupied in places (13:6b). In effect God was telling
Joshua that his service in the wars of extermination had
come to a close, and the work which he had begun
would be completed by others, God working through
them, as He had through Joshua. God's enterprise is
never limited to single individuals. The workers may die,
but the work goes on. The retirement of Joshua from
military leadership and the early division of the inheritance were divinely designed to inspire in the individual
tribes a courage and energy to complete the conquest on
their own and secure a total inheritance. God's ways
with a Christian are the same today as He warmly and
graciously encourages a weaning from overdependency
on human leaders and a pursuit of the fullness of Christ
by dealing with the personal sins and weights still lurking in the shadows.

II. SPECIAL CONCESSION (to two and one-half
     tribes) (13:8-33)

The description of the land allotted to the Reubenites,

[3]Refer to the Berkeley Version (footnotes) and *The Wycliffe
Bible Commentary*, p. 222, for help in identifying the unfamiliar
geographical terms.

the Gadites, and the half-tribe of Manasseh is given here
in Joshua to make the twelve-tribe record complete.
Joshua was merely to confirm what Moses had earlier
assigned to these tribes—an assignment that was made by
special concession. For when these tribes, who were
owners of great herds of cattle, saw the rich grazing
ground of Transjordan on the Israelites' arrival at Moab,
they asked to be assigned the land immediately (Num.
32:1 ff.). Moses at first refused, on the grounds that this
was unfair to the other tribes, who would have to fight
for their inheritance. But when assured that the two and
one-half tribes would fight for their brethren before returning to settle down in the land, Moses agreed to grant
this special favor, and so he divided the land among
them (Num. 32:33-42). (See map on page 112 for the
boundaries of the lands divided among the twelve
tribes.) The allotment to *Reuben,* at the south of Transjordan (13:15-23), was land well suited for grazing and
cultivation, as was also *Gad's* inheritance (13:24-28).
The half-tribe of *Manasseh* received the rich tableland
which included Bashan (13:29-31). The eastern boundary of all three lands was the least defined, for the simple
reason of the presence of enemy Bedouin peoples which
still held those lands.

"These are the inheritances which Moses distributed
in the plains of Moab, beyond the Jordan at Jericho, eastward" (13:32). This summary statement is significant
in view of the contrasting verse which immediately follows: "But unto the tribe of Levi Moses gave no inheritance: Jehovah, the God of Israel, is their inheritance,
as he spake unto them" (13:33).[4] The motive of the

[4]Verse 14 is related to verse 8 in the same contrasting manner.

Transjordan tribes' request was obviously self-centered, stirred by the tempting sight of things, in this case, green pasturage. But they were to pay dearly for their covetousness in the days to come, for their land was continually exposed to invasions from the Moabites, Ammonites, Syrians, Midianites, Amalekites, and other tribes of the desert, and they were the first of Israel to be carried into captivity by the Assyrians. By contrast with the desires and allotments of the two and one-half tribes, the reference to the Levites' "no inheritance" takes on spiritual significance. The appraisal of an inheritance is not by weight of gold. The Levites' "no inheritance" was not a punishment or deprivation, for, although the brothers Levi and Simeon had been cursed by their father Jacob for murder (Gen. 49:5, 7), from the moment of their later consecration to God (Exodus 32:26-29) the Levites were marked for blessing and singled out for service to God. Thus when it came time to assign land as an inheritance, no territory was sufficiently sanctified or holy for them (cf. Num. 18:9-24), hence there was "no inheritance" of land as such.[5] Theirs was a priceless inheritance, the Lord Himself. "Jehovah, the God of Israel, is their inheritance" (13:33*b*). The Christian servant of God today can ask nothing greater!

III. SPECIAL REWARD I (to Caleb) (14:1-15)

A. Introduction (14:1-5)

Moses' allotments of Transjordan having been recorded, the distribution of Canaan among the remaining tribes, made by Joshua with the help of Eleazar the priest and ten princes from the tribes (Num. 34:16-29), is now

[5]Their inheritance of cities is described in chapter 21.

the subject of the account. Since the tribe of Levi was not given an allotment of land, the writer of Joshua explains that there were still twelve tribe allocations, and not eleven, since the children of Joseph accounted for two tribes, Manasseh and Ephraim (14:4).[6]

B. Reward Claimed (14:6-12)

When the children of Israel came together at Gilgal to determine the lots for Judah and the sons of Joseph, Caleb's personal claim was considered first. Forty-five years previously Caleb and Joshua alone had given the minority recommendation to Moses to enter Canaan despite the presence of giants and fortified cities. For their faith, both were promised an inheritance in Canaan. Now Caleb steps forth from the ranks of Israel to claim his promised reward. For wholly following the Lord, he was promised land of the area where his spying journey took him, which included the hill country of the Anakim, the giants (14:9, 12; Deut. 1:36). Lest there be the objection that an aged man of eighty-five would not be capable of ousting the remnants of the powerful Anakim still dwelling in the area (for the condition of dwelling in the land was the ability to battle against any enemies located there), Caleb assured Joshua he was as strong as forty years before, and with the Lord's help would drive out the Anakim (14:10-12).

C. Reward Given (14:13-15)

Joshua, warmed by the optimistic and assuring words of his friend and former co-worker, and unmarred by any

[6]Read Genesis 48:1-6 for the origin of Joseph's double inheritance.

taint of haughtiness because he was Caleb's superior, blessed him and gave him the fields and villages of Hebron (cf. 21:12), a strategic city of the hill country, twenty miles south of Jerusalem, which had blessed associations with Israel's history from its beginning, in the days of Abraham (Gen. 13:18; 35:27). And Caleb lived up to the spirit of his determination and to Joshua's confidence in him, by subsequently driving out the enemy (15:14-17),[7] so that "the land had rest from war" (14:15).

The unwavering faith and unfailing strength of Caleb are a stirring challenge to all Christians. To many, seeing is believing, waiting is wearying, and aging is to retire. For Caleb, believing was to see Canaan conquerable; waiting through the wilderness years and the wars for Canaan was to be strengthened; and aging was to take on another giant task with the same strength-giving God. Caleb was awarded this prize in Canaan because he was committed wholly to the Lord.

IV. MAIN INHERITANCE (15:1—19:49a)

The narrative of Joshua now records the long description of the division of the land inheritances to the nine and one-half tribes. The land west of the Jordan was the real kernel of Canaan. Most of Israel's past history had been written here, and it would be so in the future. Because of the land's diversity (topography, climate, resources, commerce, locations, etc.), its partitioning could prove stimulating to each of the tribes. For each tribe could prosperously develop its own potentialities, and

---

[7]From Judges 1:9-13 one may conclude that Caleb was assisted in the battle by warriors from Judah, and that the enemy was driven out after Joshua's death.

be justly proud of its own program. The prospect of propagation of the divine truth to the heathen nations of the surrounding world from a nation of twelve strong and virile tribes, unified in spirit and faith, was tremendous—if only the threat of internal jealousy, discontent, and unbelief could be thwarted.

The basic principles of allocation had been stated originally by Moses (Num. 26:52-62), and were based on the sizes of the tribes (Num. 26:4-51) and the drawing of lots.[8] When it came time to divide the land, it was understood that the largest and most prominent tribes of Judah and the sons of Joseph should receive their land first, which would determine the remainder of the allotments to be made. The allotments for Judah, Ephraim, and Manasseh very likely were made at Gilgal. The later allotments were made at Shiloh (18:1).

A. Judah (15:1-63)

1. *Geographical Borders* (15:1-12)

Judah, the imperial tribe most blessed of Jacob's sons (cf. Gen. 49:8-12), was given a large and good land

[8]Some of the details of determining the land allocations for the seven tribes are described in 18:4-10. It is possible that the lands given to Judah and the sons of Joseph were determined in the same manner. If the size of the tribe determined the value of the parcel received, and the lot determined the geographical location, the procedure may have been: (1) on the basis of a thorough land survey, parcels of land whose value (determined by acreage, number of cities, water supply, etc.) was proportional to the size of each tribe were identified for each of the four general geographical sectors, namely, north, south, east, and west; (2) the drawing of the lot determined where the land was located; the survey had already defined the borders of the parcel for that geographical sector.

(15:1-12). Three prominent prophecies of Jacob's blessing were fulfilled in this land assignment:

Exposure to the enemies (Gen. 49:8-9). Bordering
Judah were the Moabites to the east, Edomites to the
south, Amalekites to the southwest, and Philistines to
the west. The exposure demanded a strong Judah, and
from his ranks emerged such mighty men as David.

Land of the vineyard (Gen. 49:11-12). Moses' spies
made special note of the grape produce of the area
(Num. 13:22-24).

Land of the scepter (Gen. 49:10). Jerusalem was allotted nominally to Benjamin, but it became identified
with Judah. The throne of David was eventually set up
there, and the messianic ("Shiloh"[9]) rule was associated
with it.

2. *Caleb's Battle of Extermination* (15:13-19)

Located in Judah's portion was Hebron and its environs, given to Caleb. The inclusion of this account,
supplementing the story of chapter 14, provides specific
examples of three situations confronting the tribes in
their settling down in the land:

The enemy was not easily destroyed. For whereas
Joshua and his army had destroyed the Anakim (11:21-
23), now Caleb must drive out other sons of Anak
(15:14).

The Israelites continually needed incentives to fight.
Here, Caleb offers the prize of his daughter (15:16-17).

Water supply was a determinant in the assignment of

[9]Genesis 49:10*b*. "Shiloh," literally "he to whom it [the scepter]
belongs."

land to individual families. Here, Caleb honors his daughter's request for water springs (15:18-19).

3. *Four Regions of Cities* (15:20-62)

Judah's inheritance extended over four topographically different regions: the South's dry plains (15:21-32); the western foothill bordering the coastal plain ("lowland," 15:33-47); the central ridge of hill country (15:48-60); and the sparsely populated desolate wilderness of the slopes leading down to the Dead Sea (15:61-62). The large number of cities inherited (109)[10] indicates the value of the land given Judah, for with cities were associated water supply, arable land, and defensible position.

4. *Jebusites Remain* (15:63)

This is one of the sobering aspects of Judah's occupation, a problem which the other tribes also faced. In Joshua's campaign against the five kings (chap. 10) he slew the king of Jerusalem and his army, but did not take the city at that time. Now Judah was suffering from that mistake or loss, for a strong contingent of the Jebusites had redeveloped in the meantime, and would not be driven from the city. After Joshua's death Judah smote and burned the unwalled residential area of Jerusalem's southwestern hill (Judges 1:8),[11] but, like the Benjaminites (Judges 1:21), was never able to drive out the Jebusites from the area. What was worse, children of Judah dwelt there with the Jebusites for many years to come (II Sam. 5:6-7), a fellowship which could not

[10]"The differences between the number of cities listed and the totals cited are due to inclusion or exclusion of suburbs or hamlets" (Berkeley Version, footnote).
[11]See *The Wycliffe Bible Commentary,* p. 224.

nurture a true worship of God. The city destined to be
the *holy* city was one place of Israel's inheritance which
failed of God's blessings because she harbored idolaters!

B. Sons of Joseph (16:1—17:18)

Next to Judah, the largest and most important allotment
was that made to the family of Joseph. As a reward for
Joseph's service during the early famine years, his sons
Ephraim and Manasseh were ordained to be heads of
two tribes (Gen. 48:5). The lot for Joseph's inheritance
described the fertile and beautiful land bordering most
of the Jordan River. The southern border (16:1-3) was
not contiguous with the northern border of Judah, in
order to reserve land for some of the seven smaller
tribes.[12]

1. *Ephraim* (16:4-10)

Ephraim, blessed over Manasseh (Gen. 48:19), received the land in the vicinity of many of Joshua's battles, including what was to become the sacred spot of
Shiloh. Some of its cities were located in the Manasseh
territory, an arrangement that probably was intended to
make the allotment equitable, and which no doubt served
to encourage a unity among the tribes. Like Judah with
Jerusalem, Ephraim had a thorn in its side: the Canaanites whom the men of Ephraim did not drive out of
Gezer.

2. *Manasseh* (17:1-13)

The descendants of Machir, firstborn of Manasseh, set-

[12]The northern boundary of Joseph's lands is not described in
16:1-3, since that boundary was rather indefinite, as the chapter
goes on to relate.

tled east of the Jordan. The remaining heirs, the other half-tribe of Manasseh (17:2-6) were given the large land north of Ephraim, including the beautiful plain of Shechem. By and large the region, later known as Samaria, had been sparsely populated, and this partly accounts for the book of Joshua's not recording any major battle here during Joshua's military campaigns. But its northern boundary, contiguous with those of Issachar, Zebulun, and Asher, was located in the vicinity of many strongly defended towns. Apparently for military purposes Manasseh was given some towns located in the areas of the smaller (and weaker) tribes of Issachar and Asher (17:11); but even at that "the children of Manasseh could not drive out the inhabitants of those cities" (17:12).

3. *Complaint and Solution* (17:14-18)

The complaint of Ephraim and Manasseh was strong and bitter. They felt they deserved a larger inheritance since God had blessed them with such a large population, and the habitable areas to dwell in were in their estimation too small. Joshua's answer was both a rebuke and a solution. A truly great people should be able to take the small and make it big. His solution was for them to apply brawn and cut down the wooded forest and *make* room. Then, having established themselves firmly in the hill country, they would be able to drive out the heavily armed and formidable Canaanites in the north valley regions, which threat was the basic reason for their complaint in the first place. If Judah had to deal with enemies from all sides, the sons of Joseph could not expect an easier inheritance! Joshua's closing words to them (17:17-18) were a strong encouragement and challenge, applicable also to Christians today:

"Thou art a great people,   (POSITION)
and hast great power; . . .   (POWER)
forest, thou shalt cut . . . down . . .   (TOIL)
for thou shalt drive out the Canaanites. . . ."(TRIUMPH)

C. Seven Remaining Tribes (18:1—19:51)

Most of the land of Canaan had been divided among the key tribes of Judah, Ephraim, and Manasseh. Joshua now considered it appropriate and necessary to lead his people to a spot in the middle of the possessed land, and set up the altars of worship there. In doing so he was reminding the people that the key to the blessedness of their inheritance was putting God first and worshiping Him. This principle of life has been wisely stated by someone: "Wherever I have a house, there God shall have an altar." The place chosen for this center of worship was Shiloh, about eleven miles south of Shechem, which was conveniently located in the central area of Canaan.[13] Shiloh means "rest," and it was very appropriate that at the place so named by Joshua Israel should officially enter into a new era of its life—in God's rest-land—with the land subdued before them, the larger part of the inheritance allocated, and the ceremony of commencement being a worship service in the Lord's house.

But seven tribes were still without a home, and this was Joshua's next immediate concern. Evidently the responsibility for initiating and undertaking the allocation

[13]The tabernacle remained at Shiloh for over 300 years (cf. I Sam. 4:1-11).

proceedings rested with the tribes themselves, for they were sternly rebuked by Joshua for neglecting this business: "How long are ye slack to go in to possess the land . . .?" (18:3). Their negligence in the matter very likely stemmed from the rut of nomadic and purposeless ways into which they had fallen, and from their reticence to have to take up arms again on their own, when they reached the new land. To get things going Joshua had each of the seven tribes appoint three men to a surveying committee, to divide the unpossessed land into seven portions. This was a complex, time-consuming task, but necessary for an equitable division of the land. When they delivered their survey to Joshua, he cast lots for the lands "before Jehovah," as each of the tribes learned for the first time where its home was to be. The text of Joshua proceeds to describe the geography of the lands the tribes received, in the order of the lots drawn. The chart on page 113 summarizes the pertinent facts of each allotment, and a study of it and the adjacent map will help to reveal the individual characteristics of each inheritance.

V. SPECIAL REWARD II (to Joshua) (19:49-51)

Not until all of the tribes had received their land inheritances was Joshua, their faithful and humble leader, given a parcel of land "according to the commandment of Jehovah" (19:50).[14] It was characteristic of selfless Joshua to see his people taken care of first. His choice of the land parcel also revealed his deep humility: he asked for Timnath-serah, a city in the hill country of his own

[14]God's promise, though unrecorded in the biblical text, was no doubt similar to that given Caleb (14:9).

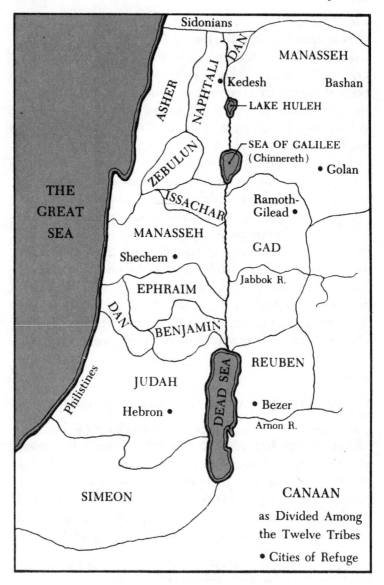

Sidonians

MANASSEH

ASHER

NAPHTALI

DAN

Kedesh • Bashan

LAKE HULEH

ZEBULUN

SEA OF GALILEE
(Chinnereth)

• Golan

THE
GREAT
SEA

ISSACHAR

Ramoth-
Gilead •

MANASSEH

GAD

Shechem •

Jabbok R.

EPHRAIM

DAN

BENJAMIN

REUBEN

DEAD SEA

Philistines

JUDAH

Hebron •

• Bezer

Arnon R.

SIMEON

CANAAN

as Divided Among
the Twelve Tribes

• Cities of Refuge

LAND ALLOTMENTS

Tribe (Number of male warriors)[1]	Location	Significance of Location	Description, Resources
Joshua 18:11-28[2] BENJAMIN 45,600	—between Judah and Ephraim	—location of holy Jerusalem —encouraged close association with Judah	—mountains and ravines —rough terrain —not productive
19:1-9 SIMEON 22,200	—part of Judah on the south[3]	—enemy exposed	—mostly flat and desert
19:10-16 ZEBULUN 60,500	—included plain of Megiddo —had access to the coast	—next to its wilderness encampment neighbor, Issachar	—fertile plain —road to sea —very productive
19:17-23 ISSACHAR 64,300	—east of Zebulun —south of Sea of Galilee	—valley of Jezreel a noted battlefield of Palestine	—beautiful location —in traffic of plain —very productive
19:24-31 ASHER 53,400	—south of enemy Sidonians —coastal land from Carmel to Sidon	—Asher's strength protected Israel from northern coastal enemies	—fertile coastal plains —famous for olives
19:32-39 NAPHTALI 45,400	—east of Asher —west of Sea of Galilee and Merom	—important lands in N.T. history	—north-south ridge through the land —fertile, productive valleys
19:40-48 DAN 64,400	—west of Benjamin —access to Great Sea	—original location too small[4] —exposed to Philistines on SW	—productive section in Philistines' hands

[1]Census taken by Moses (Num. 26:1-51).
[2]For the prophecies relating to the land inheritances, read Genesis 49 (Jacob's prophecies) and Deuteronomy 33 (Moses' prophecies).
[3]Because Judah could not manage the large land allotted to it (19:9).
[4]Eventually some daring Danites migrated to the North, settling next to Naphtali (Judges 17-18).

tribe Ephraim, on the bleak north side of the mountain
of Gaash (Judges 2:9), not a paradise rich in fertility or
beauty, but a place to build up and to dwell in (19:50*b*),
to serve the Lord and to die in (Judges 2:8-9).

VI. SPECIAL CITIES (20:1—21:42)

Now that the land was divided among the tribes,
Moses' directions for assigning cities of refuge (Num.
35:9-34; Deut. 4:41-43; 19:1-13) and Levitical towns
(Num. 35:2-8; cf. I Chron. 6:54-81) could be carried
out.

The six cities of refuge (chap. 20) were for the benefit
of the people guilty of involuntary manslaughter. The
cities were located for convenience of access, three on
each side of the Jordan River (20:7-8; see map on page
112), and served as visible reminders of God's merciful
provision of deliverance.

The forty-eight Levitical towns (chap. 21) were for
the benefit of God's servants the Levites, and constituted
their sole material inheritance of the land of Canaan,
namely, a place to live and a little pasturage. Their real
inheritance was the Lord Himself, as He had said. The
cities were purposely located throughout the regions of
all the tribes, that by the Levites' ministry of serving in
the things of the sanctuary, and walking daily in the
midst of the people, they might exalt the covenant and
laws of God and encourage the people to walk wholly
after Him.

The vital importance of the spiritual ministry of the
priests and Levites in behalf of the Israelites is clearly
described in Numbers 18:1-32. The future success of

Israel surely depended on the pervasive salting influence of these servants of God in the midst of His people.

VII. CONCLUSION (21:43-45)

This concluding statement of the *Inheritances* section emphasizes the fulfillment of God's promise up to this moment of time: "All came to pass." God had promised possession of the land, rest round about, and victory over the enemy; and in the large reference of the spirit of the words of these verses, Israel had all three. God had not failed in anything, and if Israel hoped to develop and increase the blessings of rest already received, the nation must grow in heart to a fuller knowledge and experience of Him.

* * *

Before studying the concluding *Consecration* section of Joshua, it is profitable for the reader to review the *Inheritances* section and derive some practical spiritual applications. Many illustrations may be derived from the multitude of details given in the descriptions of the allotments to the twelve tribes. Some of the large teachings suggested by the overall account are:

1. *Sovereign Location*

The procedure of lots was to emphasize the Lord's part in locating His people. Some locations were designed for chastisement (e.g., Simeon); some for reward (e.g., Judah); some for challenge (e.g., Asher with its bordering enemies). All were located with the destiny of being places where God could dwell in the midst, and reveal Himself to His people and to the world through history.

2. *Gracious Inheritance*

Every land allocation, regardless of its description, was a gift of grace, undeserved, a dwelling place for a people who up till now had no home. There was a mine of blessing located in every land.

3. *Inspiring Challenge*

Rest-land was not vacation-land. It was a land of opportunity, of proving God in the face of the enemies, of progressively growing stronger and purer in life and in worship.

4. *Beauty of Diversity*

As widely as the tribes differed one from the other in numerous respects, so the lands themselves were very diverse. This is a simple illustration of the beauty of God's working one purpose in various ways, even as the Church today proclaims the one gospel of the one God, but by different methods (I Cor. 12:5). The individuality of each tribe teaches also the warm truth of God's personal concern for each individual of His vast creation.

5. *Strength of Unity*

The division of the land was made with a view toward unity. When a weaker tribe needed auxiliary strength, its stronger neighboring tribe assumed the protectorate of bordering towns. Two intimately friendly tribes (e.g., Dan and Naphtali) sometimes were located apart from each other, to cement the union of the whole nation. The strongest bond was the one tabernacle to serve the congregation of all the tribes. The potential of a strong nation of Israel blessed of God was great, if this unity of faith and fellowship would be nurtured.

PART FOUR

CONSECRATION
(22:1—24:33)

I. CONSECRATION OF EASTERN TRIBES
   (22:1-34)
   A. Joshua's Charge (22:1-9)
   B. Tribes' Altar of Witness (22:10-34)

II. CONSECRATION OF WESTERN TRIBES
    (23:1—24:28)
    A. Joshua's Charge (23:1-16)
    B. Covenant Renewal (24:1-28)

III. APPENDIX (24:29-33)

   SUMMARY

Part Four

CONSECRATION

(22:1–24:33)

THE FIRST FIVE CHAPTERS of Joshua, the *Preparation* section, are chapters of anticipation of conquest. The last three chapters, this *Consecration* section, are chapters of anticipation of continued dwelling in God's rest-land. The intense action of the first half of the book, which reached a plateau in the business of land allotments, now gives way to relatively quiet but emotion-filled moments of crisis, when Joshua appeals for total commitment, and elicits Israel's consecration to God, a heartwarming climax to the years of his ministry among them.

I. CONSECRATION OF EASTERN TRIBES (22:1-34)

A. Joshua's Charge (22:1-9)

Commending the Reubenites, Gadites, and half-tribe of Manasseh for their faithful military assistance to their brethren the western tribes, as that assistance was stipulated by commandment of Jehovah through Moses and Joshua (22:1-3), Joshua blessed them and sent them on their way back to their own land and people, laden with

precious spoil from the battles (22:4, 6-9). But he did
not bless them without exhorting them to take diligent
heed to fulfill the conditions for continual blessing, namely, to *do*, to *love*, to *walk*, to *keep*, to *cleave unto*, and to
serve. It was a brief but passionate charge.

B. Tribes' Altar of Witness (22:10-34)

Fired by Joshua's charge and the exciting prospect of
returning home after these long weary war years, and
no doubt touched by this moment of separation from
those with whom they had lived and fought, the armies
of the eastern tribes erected a large monument or altar
by the Jordan River on its western side,[1] to symbolize the
unity between the people on both sides of the river.
The western tribes heard of the altar and, misjudging
their motives and assuming that this was an altar for
offerings and sacrifices, condemned them for the treach-
ery of disowning *the* altar of God by constructing a second one.[2] The Israelites threatened to go to war with
the eastern tribes, because they knew that God would
punish *all* Israel for rebellion even on the part of a few,
as He had done for Achan's sin (22:12-20).

Fortunately, the Transjordan people were given an
opportunity to defend their action, which they did on a
strong oath: "The Mighty One, God, Jehovah, the Mighty
One, God, Jehovah, he knoweth" (22:22). The altar,
they vowed, was not for offering, but to be a pattern of
Israel's altar, a witness to the solidarity and oneness of
Israel's faith. Then, though the Jordan divided the land

[1] *The Wycliffe Bible Commentary* suggests a location overlooking
the ford at Adam leading to the Jabbok valley (p. 228).
[2] The Israelites knew that God's prescription was for one altar
for such offerings (Deut. 12:13-14; Lev. 17:8-9).

into two parts, future generations of Israelites could not look upon the eastern people and say, "Ye have no portion in Jehovah"—for this altar would remind them otherwise (22:23-29).[3]

The explanation pleased the children of Israel, whose one concern was that the Lord would remain in the midst of all the people (22:31). The altar was called "Ed" ("witness"), for it was a witness between the two peoples that "Jehovah is God" (22:34).

II. CONSECRATION OF WESTERN TRIBES (23:1—24:28)

A. Joshua's Charge (23:1-16)

At the close of the business of distributing the land and city inheritances (21:43-45), it was understood that though Israel's enemies as a whole had been subdued, it was each individual tribe's responsibility to purge its own land of the presence of any remaining idolatrous people. Continued blessing depended on this, and so Joshua, in one of his last addresses to the people, urged their faithfulness concerning this urgent matter. The highlights of his charge were:

1. *God's help:* "He will thrust them out from before you" (23:5, 10)

2. *Israel's part:* courage; obedience to the law (23:6); separation from the life of idolatrous nations (23:7, 12, 16); cleaving unto the Lord (23:8, 11)

3. *Consequences:* possession of all the land for fulfill-

---

[3]The concern and enthusiasm of the eastern tribes in erecting such a monument is understandable, but Israel's three-times-yearly gathering at the altar at Shiloh (cf. Exodus 23:17) would accomplish the same purpose, and more indelibly.

ing the conditions; or perishing from off the land for idolatry (23:12-13, 15-16)

B. Covenant Renewal (24:1-28)

This is the last recorded ministry of Joshua to his beloved people. His dying wish was that they would burn four great impressions on their heart and in their life: covenant, history, present blessing, and consecration.

1. *Covenant*

This was the reason for gathering Israel to Shechem,[4] for this was the place that suggested the original covenant made by God with His people. Here God first promised Canaan to Abram (Gen. 12:6-7); here Jacob built an altar (Gen. 33:20); here Joshua built an altar and renewed Israel's covenant relationship with God (Joshua 8:30-35). Joshua's appeal to Israel was to rest its destiny on the foundation of the covenant. At the end of his speech on this momentous day, "Joshua made a covenant with the people . . . , and set them a statute and an ordinance in Shechem" (24:25).

2. *History*

Joshua's appeal here was to remember history. From the divine call of Israel's father Abraham to their inheritance of the land, God was the gracious Deliverer (24:2-12).

3. *Present Blessings*

"Count your present blessings" is the effect of the few

---

[4]The charge of chapter 23 very likely was made at Shiloh.

words of 24:13. Israel was now enjoying the gift of a fruitful land to dwell in.

4. *Consecration*

This was the appeal to the will, and Joshua did not intend to let the people make their choice lightly. The dialogue proceeded in this order:

a. *the clear option:* "Choose you this day whom ye will serve"—Jehovah, or the gods (24:14-15).

b. *Joshua's example:* "As for me and my house, we will serve Jehovah" (24:15).

c. *Israel's hasty commitment:* "We also will serve Jehovah" (24:18). There was no flaw in the words of this commitment. But Joshua sensed that the words probably were spoken too quickly, without due deliberation, and the words "far be it from us that we should forsake Jehovah" had the sound of dangerous self-confidence.

d. *Joshua's challenge:* "Ye cannot serve Jehovah; for he is a holy God" (24:19). The sole purpose of this strong statement was to disarm Israel's self-righteousness.

e. *Israel's deliberate insistence:* "Nay; but we will serve Jehovah" (24:21).

When Joshua was satisfied with the genuineness of the people's consecration, he solemnly renewed the covenant, laid down statutes and decrees for them, wrote the precepts in the book of God's law and, "taking a large stone, he set it up there beneath the oak tree which was sacred to the Lord" (24:26),[5] which would be a witness to the people's renewal of their consecration to God.

Joshua's earthly ministry thus came to a close. Satisfied

[5]Berkeley Version.

that his people's consecration was in earnest, he "sent the people away, every man unto his inheritance" (24:28).

III. APPENDIX (24:29-33)

The words appended to the book of Joshua recording the burial of three of God's servants—Joshua, Joseph, and Eleazar—are a fitting conclusion to the theme of the book, in the sense of what is suggested beyond their earthly lives. Canaan was given for an inheritance. But the land at most was a temporary inheritance. For Joseph, who had died in Egypt, there was only a cemetery plot in the land for his bones (cf. Gen. 50:25-26; Exodus 13:19). For Eleazar, the high priest, there had been the blessed privilege of sharing Joshua's service to God in the distribution of the land (Num. 34:17); but he died. For Joshua, there was the ministry of leading his people to serve God, a ministry that extended even beyond his lifetime, but he also died.

BUT THESE DIED IN FAITH. The rest of Canaan land, blessed as it was, was but for the short span of a lifetime. Projected into the life beyond, in the bosom of the Father, this rest would be transformed to eternal rest. Not one inheritance, but two—and this is the blessed word preached to God's people of all ages.

SUMMARY

JOSHUA'S TASK as leader of God's people was to cause them to possess the promised land. From the day of Moses' death to Joshua's own retirement and decease, his work proceeded in four movements, sequentially:

PREPARATION
CONQUEST
INHERITANCES
CONSECRATION

The days of preparation were marked by hearing the divine commission, evaluating the enemy and Israel's potential against it, seeing the mighty hand of God, identifying the leaders, mobilizing the armies, and preparing the heart for the impending holy wars.

The seven years of conquest saw God win battles for Israel, and Israel lose a battle because of sin. Joshua, fighting for God, conquered big armies and small armies, a single foe and a coalition of kings, cities in the South and cities in the North. "So Joshua took the *whole* land" (11:23).

The inheritances were the whole purpose of the wars. They were the gifts of God to His people, and no little care was devoted to their survey and distribution. These were the places where the families were to settle down to live under the canopy of God's favor.

The consecration was both inevitable and necessary. A people grateful to God for the past and the present will consecrate themselves to Him for the future. A moment of honest consecration to God their Saviour was the starting place of God's sanctifying Israel for the days to come. Joshua, in the last act of his public ministry, led the people to this moment.

SHORT BIBLIOGRAPHY
FOR JOSHUA

COMMENTARIES

BLAIKIE, WILLIAM G. *The Book of Joshua.* New York: A. C. Armstrong and Son, 1893.

BLAIR, HUGH J. "Joshua," *The New Bible Commentary.* Edited by F. DAVIDSON, A. M. STIBBS, and E. F. KEVAN. Grand Rapids: Wm. B. Eerdmans Pub. Co., 1953.

HENRY, MATTHEW. *Commentary on the Whole Bible,* one-volume edition. Grand Rapids: Zondervan Pub. House, reprinted 1961. Excellent devotional material.

JAMIESON, ROBERT, FAUSSET, A. R. and BROWN, DAVID. *A Commentary on the Old and New Testaments,* Vol. II. Grand Rapids: Wm. B. Eerdmans Pub. Co., reprinted 1948.

KEIL, C. F., and DELITZSCH, F. *Joshua, Judges, Ruth.* Grand Rapids: Wm. B. Eerdmans Pub. Co., reprinted 1950.

REA, JOHN. "Joshua," *The Wycliffe Bible Commentary.* Edited by CHARLES F. PFEIFFER and EVERETT F. HARRISON. Chicago: Moody Press, 1962. Excellent short commentary.

PHILIP SCHAFF (ed.). *Lange's Commentary on the Holy Scriptures,* Vol. 2. "Joshua." Grand Rapids: Zondervan Pub. House, n.d.

OTHER HELPS

ARCHER, GLEASON L. *A Survey of Old Testament Introduction.* Chicago: Moody Press, 1964. Background helps.

BALY, DENIS. *The Geography of the Bible*. New York: Harper and Bros., 1957.

DOUGLAS, J. D., (ed.). *The New Bible Dictionary*. Grand Rapids: Wm. B. Eerdmans Pub. Co., 1962.

GEDEN, A. S. "Joshua" and "The Book of Joshua," *International Standard Bible Encyclopaedia*, Vol. III. Grand Rapids: Wm. B. Eerdmans Pub. Co., 1952.

MANLEY, G. T. (ed.). *The New Bible Handbook*, 3rd ed. Chicago: Inter-Varsity Press, 1950. Background helps.

PINK, ARTHUR W. *Gleanings in Joshua*. Chicago: Moody Press, 1964.

REDPATH, ALAN. *Victorious Christian Living*. Westwood, N.J.: Fleming H. Revell Co., 1955. Excellent devotional messages on highlights of Joshua.

UNGER, MERRILL F. *Introductory Guide to the Old Testament*. Grand Rapids: Zondervan Pub. Co., 1951. Introductory material.

UNGER, MERRILL F. *Unger's Bible Dictionary*. Chicago: Moody Press, 1957.

Moody Press, a ministry of the Moody Bible Institute, is designed for education, evangelization and edification. If we may assist you in knowing more about Christ and the Christian life, please write us without obligation to: Moody Press, c/o MLM, Chicago, Illinois 60610.